At

Heaven's

Gate

Other titles by these authors:

- Satan's Generals – A Practical Deliverance Guide
- Deliverance Study Guide
- At Heaven's Gate
- Just Like Jesus Study Guide
- Witchcraft Xposed
- Spiritual Detox
- Tim's Travels

Just Like Him Ministries
Georgia, USA

www.justlikehim.com

Copyright notice

At
Heaven's
Gate

Foreword

Our walk with God has been filled with challenges, excitement and wonder. Imagine seeing the Creator of the Universe active in your life on a daily basis; seeing Him touch others through you in miraculous ways. This is the good news we want to share with you in this book – not only is it possible, it's what Jesus had in mind for you all along.

What makes Mark 16:17 such a special verse? It takes ordinary people, like you and me, and places us in the supernatural realm. This is where we get a firsthand experience of God's power, love and miracles. God created us to enjoy a deep and satisfying love relationship with Him. He never meant for us to be bored with Him, living in spiritual prisons, being defeated, sick and dying in torment. We want to encourage you not to be satisfied with the norm in Christianity anymore. Take a step in faith into an exciting walk with God. We did this and haven't looked back since! We find ourselves looking forward to each New Year wondering what great things the Lord is going to do this time around.

As we have walked with God, He has taught us, through His Holy Spirit, that signs will be seen in those who follow Jesus. We have chosen to believe the words Jesus spoke in Mark 16:17 and have acted on this belief. We have found that every one of these signs is available to anyone who is filled with the Holy Spirit and believes in Jesus. We drive out demons, speak in new tongues, we take up serpents daily, we have been poisoned several times but still we're alive, and we have laid our hands on many sick people and have seen them healed. We have to believe and this requires a step in faith. The same applies to these signs – you can believe that they are true, but then you have to take the step of faith, and do them.

A few months ago God asked us to write this book. His heart for us is to walk in victory and this we can only do when we follow Jesus' example. In Mark 16:17 Jesus tells us by which signs to identify His followers.

Allow this book to test and teach you concerning the signs. If you find the Holy Spirit moving your heart while you read, invite Him to teach you personally and delight yourself in Him. It's a wonderful thing to see the Lord in action in your own life and those around you. It draws you into a deep and satisfying relationship with Him. It is such a relationship with Jesus and the signs in Mark 16:17 that will ensure that you are not denied entrance to Heaven.

We pray that this book will clarify the importance and significance of signs in your life; and that it will give you the heartfelt assurance that you will meet the criteria that Jesus said is required to be recognized by Him.

You are welcome to visit the ministry website (www.justlikehim.com) for more information.

To God be all the glory.

Table of Contents

Table of Figures

INTRODUCTION

Introduction

There is one pivotal moment in our existence that is so significant that it warrants our time, attention and preparation. This moment is determined by our past, and it will affect the rest of our future. In this single moment we will reflect on our lives and Jesus will decide our future. This is the precise moment at which time has literally run out for you. No amount of excuses or pleading will change anything at this point – it will be too late! How prepared are you for this moment? Do you know the criteria Jesus will use to decide your destiny? Have you made sure that you will be recognized by Jesus as His own, or do you simply trust what others have told you? What a defining moment this is! Let's take some time to discover what Jesus had to say about this subject, and ensure that we will not be turned away from Heaven's Gate.

Let's take a virtual step into your future to that defining moment when you close your eyes for the last time and come face to face with your future. Have you thought about the different possibilities that await you at that moment? Songs have been written about it; the old and terminally ill wistfully entertain it; others dread it! How about you? Have you pictured your first face to face meeting with Jesus? Would you reach out and touch His face, or fall down in worship at His feet? One thing is for certain, this would not be the time to be wondering whether you will be welcomed into heaven or not! There is no better time than now to put this important question to rest: When you come to meet Him face to face, will you be recognized by Jesus as His own, or will you be turned away?

Making it into heaven is a big deal! The churches are full of people serving the Lord and if you were to ask any of them if they want to go to heaven, the answer would be a resounding "Yes". Yet not all of these people will be allowed into heaven. In fact very few will qualify. Are you hoping to be allowed into heaven one day? I urge you to read this book and ensure that you will be allowed in and not turned away when it's too late to do anything about it.

2

The day you approach Heaven's Gates you will not be walking beside your pastor or church leader. On that day, every person will be held accountable for their own choices. A lot of people tend to place their trust in the church leadership to ensure that they make it to heaven one day. This is a very dangerous attitude to adopt. How can I say such a thing, you ask? Here is why. The church leadership is only people, who are not yet privy to full revelation, just like you and me. What you are taught in church is therefore presented to you through a human filter. Your preacher can only give revelation to you, to the measure he, himself has received. His information will most certainly reflect the experiences he's been exposed to during his lifetime. His teachings will expose his victories and also his failures. Don't allow his failures to become your own, resulting in you standing before a closed Heaven's door.

In this book we are going to look through Jesus' eyes and see if He will recognize you as His own on the day you stand face to face with Him. In order to do this, we will be looking at Jesus' own words on this topic. We will show you how to identify a follower of Jesus. We will provide you with tools on how to measure your own success in these areas and we will also provide you with pointers on how to develop in these areas. It does not matter what church you belong to, as long as your church follows the Bible as the Word of God, this book is for you. It is based on the Bible and inspired by the Holy Spirit.

You will come across information that may challenge you in this book. We urge you to test this information with what the Bible says about it. Your eyes will be opened to areas where you and your church are lacking in knowledge or the application thereof. You might feel disillusioned in your church. You might even realize that through omission of truthful teaching, you will not be recognized by Jesus as His own.

We want to encourage you – if you are reading this, it's not too late to alter your path to lead successfully through Heaven's Gate.

3

4

CHAPTER ONE

Signs

Introduction

Mark 16:17-18, "And these signs will follow those who believe: In My name they will cast out demons; they will speak with new tongues; they will take up serpents; and if they drink anything deadly, it will by no means hurt them; they will lay hands on the sick, and they will recover."

From the earliest of times the signs of the followers of Jesus have evoked some kind of reaction in people. Some have desired the signs and have offered money to obtain them; others have denied them and called them false; while the desperately sick have reached out in hope, and others have turned away in fear and ignorance. No matter in which group you fall, when you are confronted with these signs, it will evoke a reaction in you. The signs have become a controversial issue in many churches, creating the illusion that we, as Christians, have the right to decide if it should, or should not be allowed in our lives. What do the signs you display say about you? And more importantly, what will Jesus have to say about your signs?

Have you ever asked the Lord for a sign? Have you asked God to show you which choice is the right one to make and to confirm it with a sign? You are not the first. There are several examples in the Bible of people who asked God for a sign. Gideon asked God for a sign so that he would know that God would lead him in a victorious battle against his enemy, by giving him not one, but two signs. Abraham's servant, who had to find a wife for Isaac, also asked God for a sign to help him identify the right woman. Even God Himself gives us signs to lead, comfort and assure us. The rainbow and the mark of the Beast in Revelation, are examples of God's use of signs.

I remember asking God for a sign one day. At that time, I had been the sole provider and knew that my income was crucial to the survival and wellbeing of my family. Yet I found myself trapped in a job where project after project, I had to identify people that would lose their jobs. This was torture to my soul as I knew that these people were losing their means of support for their families. For many years I justified my job by reasoning

6

that these companies survived financial hardship and could still offer employment to some. Yet at night the eyes of the hungry children would haunt me. It became so bad that, although I knew that my own family would suffer, I pleaded with God to allow me to resign.

At that time, the unemployment rate in South Africa was at 42%, which made it extremely difficult to find another job. I knew that I had to clear this move with God before I could resign. I decided to ask God for a sign of His approval. I had no idea what sign to ask for and turned to the Bible for guidance. The Lord gave me 2 Kings 20:1-11 to read. In this scripture King Hezekiah also asked the Lord for a sign and the Lord moved time back as a sign that he would be healed. So, I decided to ask God to move time back for me too. I must say, I knew it would have to be a miracle and I didn't have much faith that I would see this sign come into fulfillment. Besides, how often do you hear of time being moved back? I did however believe that God is not a minder of persons and if He did it for King Hezekiah, He could do it for me.

You can imagine my surprise, delight and leap in faith when it happened a few days later! It was announced on national TV that the world clock was being set back by one second due to some or other calculation correction that had to be done. One second was good enough for me! God gave me my sign and I was jumping for joy! I knew that God would provide for me and my family, against all odds – and He did!

God also asks us for signs. In Genesis, God required the nation of Israel to be marked with a sign. Genesis 17:11 says, "and you shall be circumcised in the flesh of your foreskins, and it shall be a sign of the covenant between Me and you." You might ask why God required circumcision. Isn't God capable of recognizing those He has a covenant with? Of course He can. So what could the reason be? Could it have been for the sake of the people themselves – a reminder for them of the covenant God had made with them? This explanation makes more sense. To display a sign requires a heart that believes and an act of faith to have the circumcision performed. The nation of Israel believed God and acted on their belief. We as Gentiles do not have to be circumcised, but we have to believe in our hearts. I will not forget the relief on my son's face when he heard the good news that he does not need to be circumcised on the foreskin any more.

Shemuel, my 10 year old son, has to read for 30 minutes every afternoon as part of his homework. We thought that this would be an ideal opportunity to turn it into a more meaningful exercise and have him read from the New King James Bible. This particular day was no exception to the rule, and he clocked in for his reading as usual. I was multitasking at that moment; working on my PC and listening with one ear to his voice as he read. There are some real nutcracker words in the Bible and Shem stumbled on one that day. The word was "circumcision". I noticed his hesitation and corrected him automatically until he asked, "So what does that mean anyway?"

It's a kind of awkward moment when this happens and you are not prepared. A lightning fast decision was reached to give a short but concise answer, and the best I could come up with was, "It's when they cut your private, as a sign that you are in covenant with the Lord". A look of shock crossed his face and a sharp intake of breath confirmed it. With a hand motion towards the relevant body part, he posed the million dollar question, "So has this been taken care of?" he asked with his wide eyes firmly focused on me. "No" I answered, sensing an opportunity for a good laugh.

The look on his face was priceless. I could literally see the pictures in his mind of the dreaded anticipated event! His whole face turned into a look of dreaded astonishment. I decided to stretch the moment for just a little longer. "Do you know Shem, when the baby boys were only 8 days old, their daddies would take a sharp rock and cut a piece of their private off!" By this time a hand was already protectively cupping the parts under threat while a look of intense pain was all over his face. He lived himself right into the story and will never forget the word "circumcision" nor its meaning! He was very relieved to hear that the Lord circumcises our hearts these days and that he won't have to be subject to it after all. God honors belief. He expects to find it in our hearts and to see us act on these beliefs, as Jesus' followers.

Jesus said in Mark 16:17 that other people will be able to identify those who believe in Him and who follow Him, because they will display the following signs: they will drive out demons, they will speak in new tongues, they will take up serpents; and if they drink anything deadly, it will by no means hurt them; they will lay hands on the sick, and they will recover. Just like circumcision, these signs are there for our benefit and a daily reminder of our covenant with God.

In this book you will be challenged to examine yourself, your place of worship and your spiritual leadership according to these signs. The motivation is not to condemn, but rather to give you the opportunity to correct those areas in which you might find yourself falling short. We pray that this book will be a blessing to you and that we will rejoice greatly with you once you have entered Heaven's gates!

What is a sign?

According to the Encarta Dictionary: English (North America), the definition of a sign is something that indicates or expresses the existence of something else not immediately apparent; something that indicates the presence of something or somebody. Based on this definition, we can conclude that the signs mentioned by Jesus are done by the working of Someone else – the Holy Spirit.

We come across signs a lot during our everyday life. An advertisement is a sign of a product being sold; a company logo is a visual sign of a company; if you see animal footprints, it is a sign of the animals presence left there; fever is a sign of an infection; in mathematic logic a sign is used to indicate operation or relation; in music different tones are represented by different signs; we even have a sign language for those who are hearing impaired and we use signatures to confirm our approval or agreement on official documentation.

In Mark 16: 17-18 Jesus states in His own words that those who believe in Him and are His followers can be identified by the following signs:
- They will cast out demons in Jesus' name
- They will speak with new tongues
- They will take up serpents
- If they drink anything deadly, it will by no means hurt them
- They will lay hands on the sick, and they will recover

Jesus gave us five distinct signs by which to measure ourselves and others to see if we are truly His followers. If you measure yourself against these signs, do you think that the Lord will recognize you as one of His followers? It's usually at this point that the defense mechanisms kick in. Many people say that not all people can cast out demons, speak in tongues or pray for healing; not to mention taking up serpents or surviving the accidental ingestion of deadly poison! This is simply not true! The quoted verses clearly state that these signs WILL follow those who believe. Signs must not be confused with the gifts of the Spirit, miracles or wonders – all of these are separate issues and mentioned as such in Hebrew 2:4, "God also bearing witness both with signs and wonders, with various miracles, and gifts of the Holy Spirit, according to His own will?"

The shocking truth in churches today is this: The truths spoken in Jesus' own words in Mark 16:17 are believed by only a few preachers and therefore seldom preached! A lot of churches are lead by people who choose to believe and preach their own views regarding Christianity and fail to preach Jesus' own words! They fear taking Jesus up on His word and accepting in faith that these things are true. Choose today to turn away from their failures and to embrace the truth of the Word of God. When you get to face Jesus, the excuse of "but my preacher failed to teach me the truth" or "I didn't know", will not be accepted.

You alone will be held accountable for the knowledge you have accumulated, your choices and your actions. The Bible states the following concerning a lack of knowledge in Hosea 4:6, "My people are destroyed for lack of knowledge. Because you have rejected knowledge, I also will reject you from being priest for Me; Because you have forgotten the law of your God, I also will forget your children." This should be a verse that puts the fear of God into all of us, but in particular, into those in leadership positions in the church. Any preacher who rejects knowledge that is taught in the Bible, such as Jesus' words in Mark 16:17, will be rejected by Jesus as His priest! If your preacher is selective about the signs, he has already been rejected by Jesus as His priest! Explore the knowledge contained in this book, meditate on it and ask the Holy Spirit to give you revelation concerning these things.

When looking at the definition of the word "sign" it becomes apparent that someone else or something else is in operation. In the case of the followers of Jesus it refers to the Holy Spirit. This becomes clear when we read John 7:38-39 where it says, ""He who believes in Me, as the Scripture has said, out of his heart will flow rivers of living water." But this He spoke concerning the Spirit, whom those believing in Him would receive…" Is it not a wonderful relief to know that you are not the one who has to work the signs? Our responsibility here is to believe in Jesus and to be filled with the Holy Spirit. It is the Holy Spirit who will work the signs through you when you step out in faith and display them. If you have problems being baptized with the Holy Spirit, examine your belief in Jesus and you'll find your problem there. This scripture clearly states that those who believe in Jesus will receive the Holy Spirit.

Many churches do not believe in the signs done through the work of the Holy Spirit. They deny their own members the opportunity to go through deliverance, thereby denying them the opportunity to live a life of victory over Satan and his demons. Instead, these people are living in bondage, imprisoned by sin, suffering and dying without any hope. They are also deprived of being witnesses to the amazing power and glory of God through deliverance. Many churches also do not believe in speaking in tongues, thereby robbing their own members of being edified in the Spirit and they stem the flow of the Holy Spirit amongst His own people. Other churches do not believe in prayers of healing, condemning their members to physical torment and hopelessness.

The main inspiration behind the churches that deny the signs of the Holy Spirit, is Satan. Satan knows that if he can keep the people from believing Jesus and from displaying the signs (as discussed in Mark 16:17), they are powerless, defenseless and easy to destroy and torment. Satan targets the church leadership and attacks them through deception and lies concerning the truth. Should the leadership lack Biblical knowledge and revelation through the Holy Spirit, it leads to omissions in Biblical teaching. Such preachers are particularly resistant to the flow of the Holy Spirit in the church. Imagine, a church where they preach God, but His own Spirit is not welcome there!

Why do we have signs

As Identification
Believers are identified by the signs they display. Signs also stir up belief in new believers. In Mark 16:17 Jesus says that His followers will be known by the signs they display. Not only do we have to display these signs but we should also measure others according to them. Have you measured yourself according to these signs? Have you measured your church leaders according to these signs? Can you identify them as Jesus' followers according to the signs Jesus said we should display? If not, you should flee from such leaders. They do not follow Jesus and they will be turned away from Heavens' door. Chances are that they will try to take many others on the same road they travel. Do not follow them into hell – there is no escape from it and the torment lasts forever!

The church leaders constantly tried to identify who Jesus was. In Matthew 12:38-39 they asked Jesus for a sign, "Then some of the scribes and Pharisees answered, saying, "Teacher, we want to see a sign from You." But He answered and said to them, "An evil and adulterous generation seeks after a sign, and no sign will be given to it except the sign of the prophet Jonah."" This sign that Jesus referred to was His death and resurrection. Here Jesus states clearly that NO other sign will be given to those who have no belief in Him. There are many church leaders today who do not receive any other signs other than the death and resurrection of Jesus. They do not receive nor display signs due to their unbelief in Jesus.

The church leadership in Jesus' time also attacked the signs that He displayed. When Jesus cast out demons, they accused Him of driving out demons by the ruler of the demons. Most church leaders today fail to drive demons out of those in their congregation. Instead they attack those who do, in the same manner that the Pharisees attacked Jesus when He delivered people. It makes you think doesn't it? What is happening in your church – is it lead by people who display the signs Jesus displayed, or are they fighting against these same signs?

13

On several occasions, when Jesus healed someone, the church leaders tried to show how Jesus broke the Biblical laws, as is evident in Luke 6:7, "So the scribes and Pharisees watched Him closely, whether He would heal on the Sabbath, that they might find an accusation against Him." In Luke 5:21 the Pharisees implicated Jesus as a blasphemer, "And the scribes and the Pharisees began to reason, saying, "Who is this who speaks blasphemies? Who can forgive sins but God alone?"" Will Jesus and His signs be welcome in the church you attend? If not, it stands to reason that your church, and the lack of signs they display will not be welcome where Jesus rules.

To Stir up belief / faith
What is belief and what does it mean to believe? Belief means to accept that something is true and it will require one to act in accordance with that belief, even if there is no absolute proof of its existence or reality.

Belief in Jesus, His words and teachings, is crucial to our salvation. Many people have a lot of knowledge of the Bible and claim to be followers of Christ, but lack the faith and belief in Jesus and His teachings. Jesus says that such people will be cast out into the outer darkness. Read what Jesus has to say about this in Matthew 8:12-13, "…But the sons of the kingdom will be cast out into outer darkness. There will be weeping and gnashing of teeth. Then Jesus said to the centurion, "Go your way; and as you have believed, so let it be done for you." And his servant was healed that same hour."" Isn't this an eye-opener; many people consider themselves sons of the kingdom, but because they do not believe Jesus and act on what He taught, they will not be allowed into heaven! Please don't let this be you – if you do not believe in what Jesus taught, ask the Holy Spirit for revelation.

God equipped Jesus to walk in signs and wonders because He knew we needed signs to convince most of us to believe. Signs are wonderful and the crowds of people who flock to witness these signs, testify of this. In John 4:48 Jesus says people believe when they see signs, "Then Jesus said to him, "Unless you people see signs and wonders, you will by no means believe.'" People also follow after signs. This is the bait on the hook of the fishers of men. Jesus was the first to draw great multitudes because of the signs He did, as seen in John 6:2, "Then a great multitude followed Him, because they saw His signs which He performed on those who were diseased."

Jesus' first sign was done in Canaan when He turned the water into wine. Jesus manifested this first sign and it led to his disciples believing as is seen in John 2:11, "This beginning of signs Jesus did in Cana of Galilee, and manifested His glory; and His disciples believed in Him." If we follow in Jesus' footsteps, we will also display our first signs amongst our family or spiritual family – an environment where we feel safe and comfortable. It is also important to display signs in our immediate family, especially as parents. This leads to belief in other family members and not only strengthens their faith but gives them the boldness and courage to flow in signs themselves. After all, displaying these signs should be a natural way of life for us, rather than being the exception in our everyday lives.

I remember the first time I heard people speaking in tongues. At that time I was not yet filled with the Holy Spirit, and being raised in a church where the signs were not encouraged, I couldn't understand what was happening. I thought the people were rather strange and I became cautious, mainly because I did not have any knowledge of this sign. It was years later, while I was at university, that I once again came across it in a Bible study group I attended. This time I was intrigued. The Holy Spirit stirred my heart and I knew that I had come across something I had been searching for, for a long time. In this group I saw and felt life, I heard testimonies of miracles and saw them happening in front of my own eyes. Intrigue changed to a burning desire to move into a deeper relationship with God. I asked the group to pray for me to be filled with the Holy Spirit, which they did. Nothing significant happened at the time and I felt a bit disappointed. Somehow I thought that all the signs would be evident right from the start, but they weren't. I didn't give up hope, but continued to attend the group, hoping that I would at least be speaking in tongues soon.

I was very impressed with the Spirit of Life that manifested in our group meetings and I found myself talking about the Lord to all my friends, testifying of the great meetings we had and inviting them to join us. On one such occasion, one of my friends committed His life to the Lord. Emboldened by his commitment, I asked the group leaders to pray with me to receive my tongue from the Lord. Most of the time, it takes a huge step in faith to start speaking in your tongue. The group leader prayed with me and then encouraged me to open my mouth and to speak. I opened my mouth but no sound came out. There I sat with my open mouth and my pounding heart! My mind attacked my faith and I briefly wondered if I would ever speak in tongues. The group leader then started praying in tongues and invited me to make a few sounds myself. I listened to the sounds she made and copied two or three of the words she said. Then it happened! My spirit soared with God and a beautiful fluent tongue rolled off my lips for what seemed like hours! I knew that there was no way on earth that I could do this out of my own. I knew that the Spirit of God prayed through me and as He did so, He filled me with new life and a deep, sure belief in God.

Parents, do not neglect the spiritual growth of your children, no matter how young they are. They must also flow in signs, there is no age restriction placed there by the Lord. My daughter must have been about four years old when, after a church service, she approached me with a very uncomfortable question. "Mommy, the people at the church asked when mommy is going to pray with me to receive my tongue?" I was quite taken aback that I did not think of it myself! At that stage, I had never prayed with anyone to receive their tongue and the only knowledge I had to go on, was my own experience when I had received my tongue. I remember looking into her eyes and noting the trust and faith she had that neither I, nor the Lord could ever fail her. It was an amazing experience for me. Hardly had I asked the Lord to fill her with His Spirit and to release her new tongue to her, when she was praying in tongues right alongside me!

After belief had been established in Jesus' disciples, He taught them how to become like Him. He specifically trained them on how to deliver others from demons. In Mark 16:20 we read, "And they went out and preached everywhere, the Lord working with them and confirming the word through the accompanying signs." Jesus proceeded by training an additional group of 70 others in deliverance. He then overcame death, went to heaven where He obtained the promise of the Holy Spirit and poured it out as described in Acts 2:33, "Therefore being exalted to the right hand of God, and having received from the Father the promise of the Holy Spirit, He poured out this which you now see and hear." After the Holy Spirit was poured out on the disciples, they spoke in new tongues, they preached the gospel and thousands believed in Jesus. They boldly cast out demons and prayed for healing for many people. They survived horrible persecution yet they did not die, until God permitted them to rest. They truly became like Jesus, even raising the dead. None of the requirements of Jesus have changed. Today we are called to be like Him and be recognized by all the things that He did.

Jesus did not only train His disciples, but he also ministered to others as can be seen in John 2:23, "Now when He was in Jerusalem at the Passover, during the feast, many believed in His name when they saw the signs which He did." Jesus' signs did not only convince the Jews, but also people from other nations. An example of this is the level of belief the centurion displayed when he asked Jesus to pray for the healing of his servant. In the same way, we should not just display the signs of our belief in Jesus to those we love and feel comfortable with, but also to others to bring them to a place of belief in the Lord.

We once ministered to an evangelist who seemed uncomfortable from the moment he set foot in our house. God warned us beforehand that we would be opposing a religious spirit during our counseling session, and it was very interesting to note how this demon manifested with fruits exactly the same as the Pharisees did in Jesus' time. The Pharisees constantly questioned Jesus about who He was and tried to get Him to contradict the Word of God. We patiently shared the Word and testimonies with this man in an effort to set him at ease concerning our faith. Through our testimony it was easy to see that we were blood washed children of God who minister based on the Bible. However, it wasn't long before the religious spirit manifested by saying, "How do I know who you are? There is no real way to test and make sure that you really belong to God!" It was quite shocking to hear such a statement coming from the lips of someone who was actively preaching God's Word. What does he teach others, if he doesn't know what a follower of Christ looks like?

To Increase the Fear of God
Another reason why we need to have the signs mentioned by Jesus is to develop a healthy fear of God. Acts 2:43 says, "Then fear came upon every soul, and many wonders and signs were done through the apostles." The fear that these people experienced was kindled because they realized how awesome God's power is. I want to make a statement based on my own experience. You will not experience a true fear of God unless God teaches it to you personally. The reason why I say this is because only the Holy Spirit can reveal God in all His power and glory to you in such a way that the magnitude of it creates a sense of awe, reverence and worship.

The fear of God is the beginning of wisdom and a subject that is not preached or taught often enough. Most of us know that we should fear God because He is Almighty and can wipe us off the face of the earth if we persist in our sins. There is a side of the fear of God that most of us are not familiar with. Did you know that there is a multitude of blessings that God releases on you when you fear Him? There are 123 scriptures in the Bible that speak of blessings that will be released on you if you fear God. Just to mention a few, these blessings and promises include that the Lord will lift up a standard against your enemy; the Lord will help you, provide food for you, give you wisdom and understanding; He will be merciful towards you; He will be your strength and will show you which way to go and He will give you favor with man. The fear of God will also keep you from evil.

I had been a diligent churchgoer for decades and I was never taught about the benefits of fearing God. Looking back I can understand the preachers' predicament. They have to work so hard to get the people to come to church that they don't want to lose them by preaching "bad" news; besides who enjoys fear? The failure to teach the flock about the fear of God, robs them of blessings and robs God of the reverence and worship due to Him. If people are not taught to fear God their attitude toward God is one of "buddy-buddy" and not of Father and son. This is a recipe for disaster and the pitfalls of this can be seen in families where the parents try to be friends to their youngsters, instead of parents. These relationships are marked by disrespect, lack of discipline and rebellion. We are not equal to God, we are created beings and God is the Creator. He has chosen the relationship between us to be that of a Father and son. As such, He carries the responsibility in this relationship. We are the dependant ones and it's in our best interest to honor this relationship.

For those of us who grew up with a father in the house, we know that it's enjoyable in the house when we obey Dad's rules. On the other hand, we know that if we break the rules, all kinds of unpleasant things happen. The same applies to our relationship with God. Our eyes should constantly be on our Father to see if He is still happy with our spiritual growth and walk. We need to make sure we follow His laws, not out of fear of punishment, but out of respect and love for the relationship and favor we enjoy with Him. If you are anything like me, when things go wrong in your life, you would be examining yourself to see what rules you have broken. As a rule, this is a good thing to do, but we also need to realize that God is a teacher and will allow trials and tribulations on our path to teach us. I would encourage you to ask God to teach you on how to fear Him. The benefits by far outweigh the pain of the lessons. I asked God to teach me to fear Him and as time went by, I forgot about my request. God did not forget and when I was totally unaware, He taught me to fear Him.

My grandmother had died of breast cancer. My mom was still young at the time when her mother's diagnosis was made known and it made a big impression on her. She spoke about it quite often and I could hear the fear of this illness in her voice. This together with medical assumptions that these kinds of illnesses are passed down the generations, always lingered in my mind. To add to this, I read a book on spiritual causes for illnesses and discovered that conflict in the mother-daughter relationship was linked to breast cancer. Although my relationship with my biological mother was good, the relationship with the woman who trained me in spiritual warfare, and whom I considered to be my spiritual mother, was not good. It was at this time that a medical examination and x-ray revealed a spot on my lung or breast. I was sent for further tests. At this point I should mention that I went for an examination because all the lymph nodes on the right side of my chest and under my arm where swollen and painful. Satan was very quick to remind me of the family history and I feared the verdict. I had two young boys at home who still needed me and I was not ready to die.

Fear is a terrible thing. If you allow it to, it can consume you. At first it felt like an information overload and I felt paralyzed by fear. The Lord allowed me to wallow in fear for a few days and then, in a very small voice, the Holy Spirit started popping questions into my head. "Who is really in charge here?" I paused. Life comes from God and only He can determine the end of it. I immediately felt better. God is in control, no matter what anyone else has to say. If I had done everything that God wanted me to do here on earth, I wanted to go home to the Lord. Besides, my children belong to God and He can take better care of them than I can. I had long discussions with the Lord about all of this and felt more positive and at peace after each discussion. The overriding impression throughout this whole experience was that our every breath is ordered by God. He is in control to such an extent that you will not die one breath before or after you should. His control is awesome. He maintains the heavens and the beauty thereof for our pleasure and as a display of His magnificence. Yet He knows the number of hairs on your head, even though you don't. He is so awesome, that He is worthy of fear, respect, reverence and worship.

God used this experienced to train me in the fear of God. All the ungodly fears I entertained turned out to be nothing but a smokescreen to keep my eyes from the power of God. Once the

Holy Spirit helped me to focus on my Savior, the truth was revealed and I was set free from ungodly fear and thoroughly immersed in Godly fear! Jesus teaches us about fear and in Luke 12:4-5, He says, "And I say to you, My friends, do not be afraid of those who kill the body, and after that have no more that they can do. But I will show you whom you should fear: Fear Him who, after He has killed, has power to cast into hell; yes, I say to you, fear Him!"

To Grow in Boldness

We grow in boldness when we constantly display the signs. Acts 4:29-31 confirms this, "Now, Lord, look on their threats, and grant to Your servants that with all boldness they may speak Your word, by stretching out Your hand to heal, and that signs and wonders may be done through the name of Your holy Servant Jesus." And when they had prayed, the place where they were assembled together was shaken; and they were all filled with the Holy Spirit, and they spoke the word of God with boldness." Do you lack boldness to speak about God? Constantly displaying the signs will embolden you to pray for others, to teach and preach and to become a conduit for God's living water to flow to those in need. Acts 14:3 also confirms this, "Therefore they stayed there a long time, speaking boldly in the Lord, who was bearing witness to the word of His grace, granting signs and wonders to be done by their hands."

I remember the times when I used to hate having to speak in front of others. At times during our schooling we were required to make speeches – these were times of intense fear and anxiety for me. I would be fearful of forgetting my words. It was a fear that made my knees shake, caused my breathing to be shallow and my body to sweat. All I wanted to do at such times was to bolt and run away as far and fast as I could. Never in my wildest imagination would I have imagined myself being called by God to stand up in front of many people to teach and preach. Well God surely did a miracle! I still consider myself to be a quiet person but when the zeal of God and His Spirit comes upon me, the words just flow and won't stop, to the point where I have even been called a preaching machine by a pastor, in whose church I preached.

Boldness to teach or preach comes when the Holy Spirit alights upon you. It's such an awesome experience to feel the fire of God inside of you, bursting forth like a powerful river after torrential downpours! There is nothing you can do to stop it and it's best to go with the flow! The Bible speaks words of encouragement, to those who lack boldness. Luke 21:14-15 says, "Therefore settle it in your hearts not to meditate beforehand on what you will answer; for I will give you a mouth and wisdom which all your adversaries will not be able to contradict or resist." God will give you the words you need to say, at the time you need to say them. In this scripture we are also encouraged to address the concerns in our hearts – which are usually anxiety, fear and a lack of boldness.

To ask God to be filled with His Holy Spirit already requires a measure of boldness. This is however only the first step in many on the path the Lord will be leading you. To follow the Lord Jesus and to become like Him, will require you to grow in boldness. There is no way that you can follow Jesus and those around you do not know it. Jesus was a public figure who caused a stir wherever He went. Either people flocked after Him or they tried their best to kill Him. If Jesus lacked boldness and hid away in a cave, we would not have been saved! We are called to become more and more like Jesus. This will require you to grow in boldness as you are led by the Holy Spirit. You will find yourself experiencing God's heart concerning certain issues or situations and all of a sudden you will not be able to stop the flood of Godly words or Godly acts that will flow. God is not a minder of persons; if He could do it for me, He most certainly will do it for you. Please ask Him daily to help you grow in boldness.

To be Edified
1 Corinthians 14:4 says, "He who speaks in a tongue edifies himself". So what does it mean to be edified? It means to be enlightened, informed, instructed, educated, improved and taught by the Spirit of the Lord. The word "enlightened" can be explained with the following image: if you are in a totally dark room and someone turns on a light, you are not just able to see everything clearly, but any fear of the unknown also flees. This

is what happens to you spiritually when you pray in tongues. Spiritual issues become clear to you; the Holy Spirit teaches you and helps you to make good choices and to grow spiritually.

There are many benefits of speaking in tongues. Let's first look at being enlightened. Have you come across issues in the Bible or in life that you do not understand? Just recently I came across something so senseless and disturbing that I could not understand it. Her name was Willemientjie Potgieter and she was only 2 years old. Willemientjie lived with her parents on a farm close to Lindley in South Africa. On 2 December 2010 five black men stabbed her daddy to death, shot her mother in front of her and then shot and killed her execution style, in the back of her head. The motive of the murder was racial, as so many others are in South Africa. The image of what had been done to this little red-head, disturbed me and I wondered what inhumane element must have been present in those who killed such an innocent, defenseless toddler. My whole being cried out to God at the injustice and wickedness of it all.

At first I struggled with the issue in my mind. This is what my mind came up with:

Willemientjie

The eagle will fly
On wings it will soar
With God she will live
And die no more

The vultures came
With a single shot
Brutally killed her
A two year old tot

And now we reel
As evil reigns
Rulers shrug their shoulders
"We're not to blame"

23

Who'll stand for justice?
Is there anyone left?
While people are dying
They're feathering their nests

Will eagles again fly
in South Africa's sky?
Will her death save others
Children die execution style?

Is this what we choose;
The legacy we leave
Death before they live
To satisfy other's greed?

This is the time
To make a firm stand
An eye for and eye
To save our land

Eagles will fly
In the skies once more
Stopping the murder
When we close the door

Death to the vultures
Who freely reign
Take back our country
And freedom again!

The human mind is carnally focused. My mind was seeking for a solution to the problem. My mind placed the blame on the criminals who killed these people, and it demanded retaliation by calling for the death penalty to be reinstated. Somehow I still did not experience God's peace and I realized that I'd not sought God's face concerning this. Here is the dialog for what the Holy Spirit answered me when I eventually communed with God to obtain His illumination and council:

God: "Do you trust me my daughter?"

Madelene: "I do Lord"

God: "Then believe that this must come to pass in order for the cup of iniquity to be filled against a nation who claimed not to be the same as your own. You see, my daughter, under the skin color, you are all the same. The white man came and took what did not belong to him. He ruled through oppression and the cries of accusation of the black man reached My ears. I turned the tables in your country and now the black man will clearly see that he is no different from the white man, and the white man will see that he is no different from the black man.

Call My people to repentance, My child, for those who are silently watching these abominations will be judged as if they committed it themselves. Call them to repentance for the cup of My indignation is full to the brim. Blood begets blood and it is not the solution to South Africa's problems. I am the Solution, turn your eyes away from your differences and focus them on Me. Invite Me back into your homes, schools, government and finances and I'll be the restorer of your country. This is a time to unite my children in prayers of repentance. Fast and pray for my mercy to be extended to you.

I've turned the tables and answered you according to the idol of racism in your hearts and you've tasted the fruit of death it has brought forth. On your request I can turn the feasting tables of the wicked to the righteous. This is in line with My will. If you seek My will for South Africa, my children must unite, regardless of color – repent and follow Me in all your ways and I will be a God to you."

As you can see, the solution that my human mind came up with differs greatly from the solution that the Holy Spirit gave me. By praying in tongues and communing with God on this issue He enlightened, informed, instructed, educated, improved and taught me through His Spirit. This example makes it clear that God's ways differ from ours and if we are not led by His Spirit we will walk in carnal and evil ways.

I'm sure we have all been challenged by issues like child molestation, poverty and major loss of life due to natural disasters which seem so unfair. And then, when we fail to come up with any good reasons with our own minds, we end up questioning God. Why is God allowing such things to happen? Many people do not receive enlightenment or information from God on these issues and turn away from their belief in God. Yet God has given us this gift to help us understand these issues and more. In fact it does so much more; it also gives us revelation into the deep mysteries of God. To shun the gift of speaking in tongues will hamper your spiritual growth as well as grieve the Spirit of God.

Have you ever experienced a situation where you genuinely do not know what to do? No matter how analytically you try and approach a problem, you still fail to come up with an answer that you know is the right one? The Holy Spirit instructs and educates you when you pray in tongues. God exists outside of time and He knows exactly which choices you need to make that will prove to be the right ones for your future. By speaking in tongues you start communing with God on a spiritual level. You fully submit your mind to God by stepping away from reasoning with your own abilities and instead, inviting God to instruct you on the way you should go. It always amazes me that people think that they are capable of understanding and explaining God and issues like speaking in tongues, yet these are precisely the issues they fail to understand or explain. They then reject them, even though the Lord Jesus Himself said it will be evident in our lives.

To speak in a tongue lifts you up into the spiritual realm and the presence of God. There is no place better to be. When you are in God's presence you are refreshed and filled with new hope and trust in Him. You also are able to face all the challenges that lie ahead of you, because you know that you do not face them in your own ability. In short you become a better person; easier to be around. Have you been around someone who is constantly negative and weighed down by problems? It drains you, doesn't it? People tend to flee from such company. The company you keep tends to rub off on you. If you keep God company, it will also rub off on you! You will become more like Him in every way. Speaking in tongues helps you to enter into God's presence more easily and the communion begins.

In 1 Corinthians 14:18 Paul says, "I thank my God I speak with tongues more than you all". Paul was probably the greatest evangelist who ever lived. He took the gospel to the gentiles and he was easily identified by all the signs Jesus mentioned in Mark 16:17. What made Paul such an excellent evangelist was that he communed with God day and night. This is a secret to spiritual greatness! He prayed in his tongue continuously. This means that the Spirit of God was interceding on Paul's behalf, all the time that Paul prayed in his tongue. Romans 8:26-27 says, "Likewise the Spirit also helps in our weaknesses. For we do not know what we should pray for as we ought, but the Spirit Himself makes intercession for us with groanings which cannot be uttered. Now He who searches the hearts knows what the mind of the Spirit is, because He makes intercession for the saints according to the will of God."

Paul placed a lot of importance on speaking in tongues and those he ministered to picked up on it. Due to their over enthusiasm, he had to lay down rules regarding the speaking of tongues, to maintain order in church gatherings. Even so, Paul thanked God that he spoke with tongues more than all those around him. If such a good example of a follower of Jesus is so thankful for this ability, shouldn't we also follow suit? So many people today allow ignorance and fear to rob them of this sign. What they don't realize is that they are also being robbed from the ability to easily enter into God's presence and to be edified.

To witness to God's Glory
Jesus often flowed in the sign of healing and it testified to the glory of God. In John 9:1-3 we read, "Now as Jesus passed by, He saw a man who was blind from birth. And His disciples asked Him, saying, "Rabbi, who sinned, this man or his parents, that he was born blind?" Jesus answered, "Neither this man nor his parents sinned, but that the works of God should be revealed in him." Then in verse 24 we see the blind man proclaiming the following: "Give God the glory!" This man was

blind from birth, not because of sin, or sins that had come down the bloodline, but he was blind his whole life in order for the miracle working power of God to be displayed openly before all.

Failure to have and display the signs which Jesus said believers in Him will have, disqualifies you from being an effective witness for God. Your witness will then only be empty words which lead to spiritual death. God confirms His works through signs, miracles and wonders as can be seen in Acts 2:22, "Men of Israel, hear these words: Jesus of Nazareth, a Man attested by God to you by miracles, wonders, and signs which God did through Him in your midst." All the works of Jesus were confirmed by God through signs, miracles and wonders. The crowds followed Him around because they knew there was something supernatural at work through Jesus. How many of us have the same problem of crowds following us around? In fact, in John 14:12 Jesus says, "Most assuredly, I say to you, he who believes in Me, the works that I do he will do also; and greater works than these he will do, because I go to My Father." Why are we not encouraged to become more and more like Jesus? Instead we accept and follow after a lesser and powerless faith that will fail to get us into heaven.

Jesus had the church leadership of His day worried! In John 11:47 we read the following, "Then the chief priests and the Pharisees gathered a council and said, "What shall we do? For this Man works many signs." The church leadership even tried to kill Jesus on several occasions. This tendency still persists today. If Jesus should walk into your church today, would He be welcomed or persecuted? Would He see the signs He mentioned in the members of your church? The same religious spirit that was evident in the Pharisees is still evident and at work in most of the church leaders today. If your church lacks the signs discussed in Mark 16:17, you are following man-made rules that are contrary to God's specifications. Flee from such a church! Not only are they robbing you from saving souls for Jesus but they will cost you your entrance to heaven – you will not be recognized by Jesus as one of His own!

We will be tested according to the spirit in which we displayed signs here on earth. If we have done the signs through the working of the Holy Spirit, Jesus will acknowledge us as His own, but if the signs were done through the spirit of the Anti-Christ, we will be rejected. The Bible says that the spirit must be tested. In 2 John 1:7 it says, "For many deceivers have gone out into the world who do not confess Jesus Christ as coming in the flesh. This is a deceiver and an antichrist." It is possible to perform signs through the Anti-Christ spirit and deceive many Christians, but it's impossible to deceive Jesus. Such deceivers will burn in hell's fire forever, and those who lacked discernment and followed after them, will spend eternity with these same deceivers.

We, as Jesus' followers, must walk in an intimate relationship with the Holy Spirit, who will expose deception and lead us on safe paths. We have to constantly examine our hearts' intentions when we flow in the signs of the Holy Spirit to ensure that we are working to glorify God and not ourselves. It will be an awful day if we find out that we have been operating in an Anti-Christ spirit when we approach Jesus at Heaven's gate and hear the words of Matthew 7:22-23, "Many will say to Me in that day, 'Lord, Lord, have we not prophesied in Your name, cast out demons in Your name, and done many wonders in Your name? And then I will declare to them, 'I never knew you; depart from Me, you who practice lawlessness!'"

Do not use Matthew 7:22-23 as an excuse not to operate in the signs. Many church leaders do this and they are robbing themselves and others of experiencing and testifying to the glory of God. In Romans 8:16 it says, "The Spirit Himself bears witness with our spirit that we are children of God." The Holy Spirit will confirm to you that you are indeed a child of the living God and not just a pretender who operates under the Anti-Christ spirit.

Below is a questionnaire to help you identify the spirit by which you operate. Read through each of these statements and mark "True" or "False".

By which spirit do I operate?		
	T	**F**
1	I believe that Jesus Christ is the Son of God		
2	I believe that Jesus lived as a man on earth		
3	I believe that Jesus died and rose from the grave		
4	I believe that Jesus is with the Father in heaven		
5	I love Jesus with all my heart		
6	I spend a lot of alone time communing with God		
7	I pray in my tongue continuously		
8	I have confessed Jesus as my Lord		
9	I have repented of all my sins		
10	I have turned away from sinful deeds		
11	I have forgiven everyone who has wronged me		
12	I give glory to God for the signs He works through me		
13	I do not expect payment for performing the signs		
14	I do not boast of the signs		
15	I do not want to receive glory		
16	I do not want to receive recognition		
17	I do not want to be worshipped		
18	I do not use signs to be in the lime light		
19	I do not perform signs to create a following		
20	I do not use signs to manipulate others		

Figure 1: By which Spirit do I operate?

If you answered "False" to any of the above statements, you have successfully identified areas of concern which you need to address. These statements focus on faith issues as well as the intentions of your heart. God does not only expect us to believe in Him, but He also expects our hearts' intentions to reflect these beliefs.

CHAPTER TWO

How do you obtain these signs?

Belief in Jesus

The first and most important requirement for you to obtain the signs is to believe in Jesus. It sounds so simple, yet many of us do not know what it means to believe! It is such a crucially important issue that it is worth making sure that we understand it fully. What does it mean to believe? A thesaurus describes the word "believe" as: to accept it as the truth; to trust in it; to have faith in it. Therefore, if you wanted to test yourself whether you believe in Jesus, you could ask yourself whether you accept what the Bible says about Jesus is the truth, that you trust in Jesus and that you have faith in Him.

Mark 16:16, 17 shows that without belief in Jesus you will not be saved, "He who believes and is baptized will be saved; but he who does not believe will be condemned. And these signs will follow those who believe: In My name they will cast out demons; they will speak with new tongues…" Many churches believe and openly confess that you have to believe and be baptized to be saved. This is true, but they should continue with the full message – that is the teaching on what a follower of Jesus will look like once they believe. Not only do they fail to teach what Jesus told us in Mark 16:17 but they also will not allow demons to be cast out, people to speak in tongues, spiritual warfare to take place or prayers of healing to be done in their churches.

One thing you clearly need to understand today is that if you do not display the signs of those who believe in Jesus as mentioned in Mark 16:17, you will not be saved! By not displaying the signs, you are displaying unbelief and hardheartedness. Mark 16:17 and John 4:48 are two scriptures that state that belief in Jesus is an essential requirement to display signs. If you believe in Jesus, all things become possible for you! Isn't this wonderful! Why is it that we limit God through unbelief? Belief is an attitude of the heart; it means that you have to become like a child and not try and work things out with your mind. Jesus said it in His own words, in Mark 9:23, "If you can believe, all things are possible to him who believes." Furthermore, Jesus encourages us to become like children who believe easily and who are humble – Matthew 18:3, "Assuredly,

I say to you, unless you are converted and become as little children, you will by no means enter the kingdom of heaven."

The following questionnaire will help you determine whether you believe in Jesus.

Do I believe in Jesus?			
		T	F
1	I cast demons out of others and myself		
2	I speak in tongues		
3	I rebuke demons who attack others and myself		
4	I have survived physical spiritual attack		
5	I have prayed for others and seen them healed		
6	I believe that Jesus Christ is the Son of God		
7	I believe that Jesus Christ lived as a man		
8	I believe that Jesus died and rose from the grave		
9	I believe that Jesus will return to the earth		
10	I trust Jesus, and I am not concerned about anything		
11	I have faith in Jesus and do not fear		
12	I have repented of all my sins		
13	I believe that when I repent of my sins, I am forgiven		
14	I believe that Jesus performed miracles		
15	I believe that Jesus cast demons out of people		
16	I have been baptized		

Figure 2: Do I believe in Jesus

If your answer to any of the above statements was "False", I strongly urge you to read up on what the Bible has to say regarding those specific statements. It is very important for you to examine the Bible on these specific issues and ask God to reveal the truth to you. The Bible clearly states that if you do not believe in Jesus, you will not enter the Kingdom of God, as stated in John 3:3, "Jesus answered and said to him, 'Most assuredly, I say to you, unless one is born again, he cannot see the kingdom of God.'"

Take the steps of obedience

The following steps of obedience are steps that must be taken in order to be born again.

Confess your belief in Jesus

The first step of obedience is to confess your belief in Jesus. This is not something that can be done without anybody else being aware of it. Romans 10:9 says, "if you confess with your mouth the Lord Jesus and believe in your heart that God has raised Him from the dead, you will be saved." So what does "confess" mean anyway? According to an online thesaurus (http://thesaurus.com), it means to: admit (own up; plead guilty, come clean, acknowledge and make a clean breast) and to make a declaration (declare; profess; affirm; assert; make known and acknowledge). A good confession with your mouth will contain all the above mentioned elements. An example of this, is:

> Dear Lord Jesus, I have sinned and I'm so sorry about it. Please forgive me and wash me clean from these sins. I turn away from committing these sins in future and ask You to be my King. Please lead my feet on paths of holiness which are pleasing to you. I confess that I believe what the Bible says about You is the truth. I believe that You are the Son of God, who has been born in the flesh. Thank you for dying for my sins. I gladly accept Your forgiveness. I confess that you have overcome death and that you have risen from the dead. I believe that you ascended to heaven and that you are seated at the right hand of the Father. I believe that you will return to take those who belong to you. Thank you, my Savior and Friend.

1 John 1:9 says, "If we confess our sins, He is faithful and just to forgive us our sins and to cleanse us from all unrighteousness." Accept this forgiveness in faith and forgive yourself and others, as you, yourself are forgiven by God.

Repentance of sins

Repentance must be a deep conviction of sin that results in rejecting past sinful behavior and adopting new Biblically approved behavior. Repentance is a powerful act that can turn God's anger away from you. Acts 26:18 says,"...to open their eyes, in order to turn them from darkness to light, and from the power of Satan to God, that they may receive forgiveness of sins and an inheritance among those who are sanctified by faith in Me."

During a deliverance session a person could be required to repent of sins committed by their ancestors. God does not automatically forgive sins. Sins have to be confessed and repentance shown. If your ancestors committed sins, they gave Satan and his demons the right to attack and inhabit them, and you. These demons, and their fruits, are passed down to the children for up to four generations. Deuteronomy 5:9 confirms this, "For I, the Lord your God, am a jealous God, visiting the iniquity of the fathers upon the children to the third and fourth generations of those who hate Me". This is what we call bloodline sins or curses. If you repent of these sins, God will forgive you and these demons may be cast out of you. This will result in an end of their fruits in your life. Nehemiah 9:2 says, "Then those of Israelite lineage separated themselves from all foreigners; and they stood and confessed their sins and the iniquities of their fathers."

As we ask God for forgiveness, we must also consciously accept it. We have found that often people have asked for forgiveness, but have not accepted the forgiveness God has given, nor have they forgiven themselves. Remember that He has washed you clean and He remembers your sins no more. It may be necessary during a deliverance session, to have the person speak out forgiveness over themselves.

Willingness to forgive

We are also expected to forgive others. Matthew 6:12 says, "And forgive us our debts, as we forgive our debtors." According to this short piece of scripture, we are required to forgive others and then we will be forgiven in the same measure that we offer forgiveness. A simple application of this principle can be found in tithing. If we have not paid tithes, we have been borrowing from God. When we go back and ask God to forgive us for not tithing or for short-tithing, He forgives us and does not expect us to pay it back, nor catch up the payments. What He does expect, is that we start to walk the path of repentance and begin tithing immediately, according to His measure.

Someone seeking deliverance must be willing to forgive anyone who sinned against them or hurt them in any way. This is crucial and we will not attempt to cast demons out of someone who does not forgive and speak it out. Jesus explains how unforgiveness will affect our own forgiveness in Matthew 6:14-15, "For if you forgive men their trespasses, your heavenly Father will also forgive you. But if you do not forgive men their trespasses, neither will your Father forgive your trespasses."

Be Baptized
The second step of obedience is to be baptized. Acts 2:38 says, "Then Peter said to them, "Repent, and let every one of you be baptized in the name of Jesus Christ for the remission of sins; and you shall receive the gift of the Holy Spirit." Baptism is a step of pure obedience. You get baptized when you realize that you have sinned and you need to turn away from an old life of sin and dirt, and arise into a new life of purity and holiness. By being baptized you lay down your fleshly life and worldly desires and enter a life in which the Holy Spirit leads you and works through you. The Holy Spirit descended upon Jesus in the form of a dove when He was baptized. Matthew 3:16-17 says, "When He had been baptized, Jesus came up immediately from the water; and behold, the heavens were opened to Him, and He saw the Spirit of God descending like a dove and alighting upon Him. And suddenly a voice came from heaven, saying, "This is My beloved Son, in whom I am well pleased." To be baptized pleases God and draws you into a deeper love relationship with Him. Even Jesus states the importance of undergoing baptism in Matthew 3:15 by saying to John, "But Jesus answered and said to him, "Permit it to be so now, for thus it is fitting for us to fulfill all righteousness." Then he allowed Him."

The Holy Spirit immediately started leading Jesus after He was baptized. Matthew 4:1 says, "Then Jesus was led up by the Spirit into the wilderness to be tempted by the devil." None of us would willingly face temptation by the devil. There is a time in one's life when you have to face those devils that have tempted you and led you into sin. This is the time in your life to do it. The devil and his demons will not be happy about your newly made commitment to the Lord. They will try their best to get you to back away from following Jesus. They will try to draw you into all the old sins you walked in prior to making your commitment to God. To you it may feel as if all hell has broken loose, but I want to encourage you, it must have felt the same for Jesus when He was tempted in the desert. He was tempted and tested on every single thing a person can ever be tempted – He made it! You will also make it if you are filled with the Holy Spirit, as your Helper and Comforter.

Go through Deliverance

Many Christians are ignorant concerning deliverance and therefore fear and avoid it. Deliverance is the first sign by which Jesus says His followers will be recognized. So what is deliverance? The word "deliverance" has a dual meaning:

- It is an act of rescue from captivity, hardship, or domination by evil

- It is also a formal announcement of a decision, judgment, or opinion

Deliverance encompasses both of these meanings. It is an act of rescue in which a person is set free in the name of Jesus Christ who came in the flesh, from those things that have kept them in captivity, hardship and being dominated by evil. Complimenting the act of being set free is the formal announcement by the person of their decision to turn from those things that gave Satan the right to keep them in bondage. As part of being saved, there is also the declaration of making Jesus the Lord upon the throne of your heart. Deliverance is a ministry of restoration and healing. When deliverance is ministered, it usually goes hand in hand with healing in the physical, emotional and spiritual areas of one's life. Luke 8:2 says, "and a certain woman who had been healed of evil spirits and infirmities – Mary called Magdalene, out of whom had come seven demons". We have seen many miraculous healings take place when demons have been cast out. Some of these testimonies we have included in our book "Who are You?" when discussing the different demonic entities.

When Jesus speaks about the importance of casting out demons, He says that the act of deliverance causes the kingdom of God to come upon you. Matthew 12:28 says, "But if I cast out demons by the Spirit of God, surely the kingdom of God has come upon you." The kingdom of God is an important aspect in a Christian's life. In all the scripture references about the kingdom of God or the kingdom of Heaven, this is the only time that Jesus says it has come upon you. All other references have the kingdom of God near to you. Jesus also gives us another important instruction about the kingdom of God in Matthew 6:33 where He says, "But seek first the kingdom of God and His righteousness, and all these things shall be added to you." By implication this means that we should seek deliverance and walk in God's righteousness and God will take care of our needs and concerns, such as food and clothing. We have taken God up on this promise on quite a few occasions and have found Him faithful in taking care of our every need and our Godly desires.

Deliverance is not the work of a few select Christians. Deliverance is something that Jesus says will identify all His followers. Mark 16:17-18 says, "And these signs will follow those who believe: In My name they will cast out demons; they will speak with new tongues; they will take up serpents; and if they drink anything deadly, it will by no means hurt them; they will lay hands on the sick, and they will recover." My question to you at this point is this: How many of your fellow believers, including yourself, cast out demons? If these are characteristics that identify His followers, how will Jesus recognize you and your fellow Christians if He does not see these signs in your lives? Does this sound harsh? Think about the idea of purchasing something by mail order. You have seen the catalog and what it should look like and be made of. Then the article arrives and when you unwrap it, you see that it looks completely different to the item in the catalog. Do you accept the article even though it looks nothing like what you wanted?

Do we ask God to accept us even though we look nothing like the signs that He said would identify us? Know for sure that the Lord will not accept this. If you cannot be identified by the signs in Mark 16:17-18, you have been robbed by Satan. Our God has been, is and always will be the Almighty God – powerful beyond measure. You, as His vessel on earth, must flow in His power!

Be thirsty for more of Jesus
John 7:37-39 says, "On the last day, that great day of the feast, Jesus stood and cried out, saying, "If anyone thirsts, let him come to Me and drink. He who believes in Me, as the Scripture has said, out of his heart will flow rivers of living water." But this He spoke concerning the Spirit, whom those believing in Him would receive; for the Holy Spirit was not yet given, because Jesus was not yet glorified."

The abovementioned scripture says that Jesus cried out when He said these words. To cry out about something shows that you are passionate and deeply emotional about it. If you want to be filled with the Holy Spirit, your heart needs to reflect Jesus' heart concerning this matter. You have to cry out to Jesus from a thirsty heart, to be filled with the Holy Spirit. It's important to note that Jesus is the One who baptizes with the Holy Spirit and when you want to be filled with the Holy Spirit, your request will be to Jesus and not to the Father.

Be filled with the Holy Spirit
The Bible is quite clear on this issue – if you are not filled with the Holy Spirit, you do not belong to Jesus and will not gain entrance to His Kingdom. Romans 8:9 says, "But you are not in the flesh but in the Spirit, if indeed the Spirit of God dwells in you. Now if anyone does not have the Spirit of Christ, he is not His." You will have a deep, heart-felt conviction if you are filled with the Holy Spirit and you will display the signs that Jesus mentioned in Mark 16:17. If you do not have a deep heart-felt conviction and you do not flow in the signs, contrary to what

others tell you, you are not filled with the Holy Spirit. You need to carefully examine this book to determine what you have to do to ensure that you will be recognized by Jesus, at Heaven's gates.

Nothing in the spirit realm happens automatically. However, where rights have been given or an invitation extended, it will manifest. Where the Holy Spirit is concerned, He will never force Himself on you. He can be likened to a gentleman, who knocks until the door is opened to Him. You will know when the Holy Spirit is knocking on the door of your heart. His gentle knocking will tug at your heart and create a burning need to move into a deeper relationship with God. You will not be satisfied with any dead religion anymore but you will have a thirst for true life and a true relationship with God. This is the heart attitude that God honors and rewards with the gift of His indwelling Holy Spirit.

In Luke 11:13 it says, "If you then, being evil, know how to give good gifts to your children, how much more will your heavenly Father give the Holy Spirit to those who ask Him!" It is in God's perfect will that we are filled with His Holy Spirit. God knows that we need the guidance and help of the Holy Spirit to grow in holiness and to overcome the enemy. The Holy Spirit is more than a good gift; it is a necessity for a follower of Jesus. Without the Holy Spirit it is impossible to face Satan and his demons and come into a place of victory over them. The Holy Spirit guides us, teaches us and gives us the power, when we need it.

Jesus trained his disciples personally, but to reach the entire world throughout all time would require spiritual intervention – the Holy Spirit. He therefore had to fulfill His calling in order to receive the promise of the Holy Spirit from the Father. Once He received this "Promise" from the Father, Jesus poured it out on His followers as is seen in Acts 2:33, "Therefore being exalted to the right hand of God, and having received from the Father the promise of the Holy Spirit, He poured out this which you now see and hear." It becomes clear that those who are filled with the Holy Spirit, witness to God in ways that others can clearly see and hear!

The signs are imparted to a believer through the indwelling of the Holy Spirit. Have you ever wondered if you are really filled with the Holy Spirit? You could test yourself to see if the signs are evident in your life. It is important to evaluate your everyday life because there are times when you are in the presence of such wonderful anointing that you start to display some of the signs purely due to the anointing. This happened to Saul when he met up with a group of prophets and then started prophesying himself.

We are called to display the signs constantly. In 2 Corinthians 13:5 Paul says, "Examine yourselves as to whether you are in the faith. Test yourselves. Do you not know yourselves, that Jesus Christ is in you?--unless indeed you are disqualified." Below is a questionnaire that will help you identify whether you are filled with the Holy Spirit. Read through each of these statements and mark "True" or "False"

Am I filled with the Holy Spirit?			
		T	F
1	I believe that Jesus Christ is the Son of God		
2	I believe that Jesus Christ came in the flesh and died to pay for my sins		
3	I have confessed Him as my Lord		
4	I have forgiven everyone who has wronged me		
5	I have repented of all my sins		
6	I have turned away from sinful deeds		
7	I have been baptized		
8	I have been delivered		
9	I have invited the Holy Spirit into me		
10	Elders have prayed for me for infilling of the Holy Spirit		
11	I am hungry for more of God		
12	I trust in God's goodness		
13	I want an intimate relationship with God		
14	I display some of the signs mentioned in Mark 16:17 (New tongues, cast out demons, healing, etc.)		
15	I have a river of life flowing from me		

Figure 3: Am I filled with the Holy Spirit?

43

If you answered "False" to any one of the above statements, I strongly urge you to read up on what this book has to say on those specific issues in the chapters to follow. It is very important for you to examine the Bible on these specific issues and ask God to reveal the truth to you. The Bible clearly states that if you are not filled with the Holy Spirit, that you will not enter the Kingdom of God!

Display signs with boldness

Once you are filled with the Holy Spirit you need to constantly measure your spiritual walk according to Jesus' example. It's important that we measure ourselves against the standard God gave us in Jesus. This makes it easier to identify where we fall short. Once we have identified those areas that need attention, we must find out why we fall short and then do something about it. Below is a list of statements pertaining to the works and signs Jesus walked in which He expects us to display. This questionnaire will help you determine to what measure the Holy Spirit works through you.

Read through each of these statements and rate yourself using a score between 1 and 5. List your scores, then add them and divide the total by the number of statements -- for example; if your total is 60, then your score will be 60/15 = 4.

1 = Never   2 = Seldom   3 = Usually   4 = Often   5 = Always

The Holy Spirit flowing through me		1	2	3	4	5
1	I drive out demons in Jesus' name					
2	I heal the sick in Jesus' name					
3	I speak with new tongues					
4	I heal the brokenhearted in Jesus' name					
5	I receive revelation from God					
6	I speak words that bring life to others					
7	I preach good tidings to others					
8	I resist the devil					
9	I walk in victory over sin					
10	I proclaim liberty to the captives					
11	I proclaim the opening of the prison to those who are bound					
12	I comfort all who mourn					
13	I see the Spirit of the Lord give those who mourn beauty for ashes through me					
14	I see the Spirit of the Lord give those who mourn the oil of joy through me					
15	I see people receive the garment of praise in the place of the spirit of heaviness when I minister in Jesus' name					

Figure 4: The Holy Spirit flowing through me

Here is what your score reveals about you:

- If your score is between 1 and 2:

You have a lot of personality of your own (self will) and you need to be poured out like water to be purified. Dying to self is never easy, nor is it a pleasant experience. The upside is even better -- you can become like Christ, walking in His image, His works and His authority. The less of you there is, the more the Holy Spirit can fit into you, bringing life to those who are dying.

- If your score is between 3 and 4:

Well done. You are well on your way on the path of holiness with the Lord. Read through the information for those whose score was between 1 and 2, and make sure that you follow the same principles and help others to enjoy a deep and meaningful relationship with God.

- If your score is 5:

Excellent! You surely shine the Lord Jesus in all you do, say and are! Please help those around you to obtain victory in this area.

Should signs be tested

If we lived in a perfect world without an enemy in sight, my answer to this question would be "No". Unfortunately we have an enemy who has been around for much longer than we have. He knows our weaknesses and he takes sadistic pleasure in attacking us on them. Satan is called the great deceiver and, where signs are concerned, he has lived up to his name! Is it possible that Satan could deceive a person to such an extent that they fully believe that they are doing God's work and will, yet they are actually under Satan's influence, caught in webs of deceit? In Matthew 7:21-23, we see people who flowed in signs, being denied by the Lord, "Not everyone who says to Me, 'Lord, Lord,' shall enter the kingdom of heaven, but he who does the will of My Father in heaven. Many will say to Me in that day, 'Lord, Lord, have we not prophesied in Your name, cast out demons in Your name, and done many wonders in Your name? And then I will declare to them, 'I never knew you; depart from Me, you who practice lawlessness!'"

How is it possible that people who prophesy, cast out demons and do wonders in Jesus' name are denied by the Lord? I believe the answer lies in Jesus' declaration to them – they never knew Him. These people never crowned Jesus as the Lord in their lives and subsequently, never did the will of the Father. Are you sure that you won't be one of these people? This scripture has niggled at the back of my mind for many years. What if, despite my deep love for the Lord, I've somehow been deceived to such an extent that I know within myself that I belong to Him, yet arrive at Heavens' Gate, to be turned away? I can hardly imagine something more horrific!

God is so good! He was fully aware that this fear attacked me every now and again. A while back, during a praise and worship service, I heard His audible voice putting these unfounded fears out of my life. "I love you, My daughter." They were simple words but exactly what I needed. He called me His daughter and I knew that He would never be able to say to me that He did not know me – because He, Himself had called me His daughter!

Review the following statements and determine whether you know Jesus in such a way that He will recognize you as one of His own. Read through each of these statements and rate yourself answering "True" or "False".

Do you know Jesus?			
		T	F
1	I believe firmly in the truth and certainty of Jesus		
2	I have invited Jesus to be my King		
3	I have been baptized by the Holy Spirit		
4	I flow in the signs described in Mark 16:17		
5	I hear God's voice		
6	I enjoy daily communication with the Lord		
7	I am deeply aware of the Lords presence and anointing		
8	I regularly submit decisions to God for His guidance		
9	I do what God tells me to do		
10	I have information concerning Jesus firmly in my mind or committed to memory		
11	I am in a deep and intimate love relationship with God		

12	My heart is not to sin		
13	I recognize differences between those who belong to Jesus and those who do not		
14	Others recognize Jesus in me		
15	God has personally told me that I belong to Him		
16	I wait on guidance from the Holy Spirit, before I minister		

Figure 5: Do you know Jesus?

If you do not positively identify the above statements as evident in your life, you need to work on them. Meditate on what the Bible has to say about these issues and ask the Holy Spirit to give you revelation. Do not allow the Deceiver to keep you from the truth, robbing you of an eternity with the Lord.

In 2 Thessalonians 2:9-12 Paul clearly states that Satan will display signs, "The coming of the lawless one is according to the working of Satan, with all power, signs, and lying wonders, and with all unrighteous deception among those who perish, because they did not receive the love of the truth, that they might be saved. And for this reason God will send them strong delusion, that they should believe the lie, that they all may be condemned who did not believe the truth but had pleasure in unrighteousness." It is therefore very important to test the spirit of those who display signs. Do they pray in the name of Jesus? What is their motivation for the signs they display? Is it bringing glory to the Lord or do they claim the fame? Do they require payment for what they do? Is what they do Biblically founded? Can you see God in what's happening and does the Holy Spirit inside of you confirm that it is right?

Now that you know that signs must be tested and not just blindly accepted, you need to make very sure that you do not reject or turn away from displaying these signs because of fear. Fear is not from God and, given the opportunity, will rob you of your eternal time with God. Jesus said that we have to have these signs – constantly ensure that your heart's motivation is still Godly and run with the signs! Enjoy them, give freely, even provoke others to jealousy if you have to…but do not quench the Holy Spirit by holding back!

CHAPTER THREE

Jesus as our perfect example

Introduction

Luke 4:18-21, "The Spirit of the Lord is upon Me, because He has anointed Me to preach the gospel to the poor; He has sent me to heal the brokenhearted, to proclaim liberty to the captives and recovery of sight to the blind, to set at liberty those who are oppressed; to proclaim the acceptable year of the Lord."

In Isaiah 61:1-2 and Luke 4:18-21 Jesus' commission on earth is described. In these scriptures it is easy to see that Jesus has been anointed and sent to heal and deliver. Jesus is therefore not asking us to do anything that He has not done Himself. We are called to follow Jesus' example.

In Jesus' last words to His followers on earth, He told us by what signs His true followers would be recognized. The question can now be posed: If we look back at the Biblical account of Jesus' time here on earth, can we recognize these signs in Jesus?

According to His teachings, He came to conquer sin to give us the opportunity to choose whether to display behavior resulting in blessings or curses in our lives. Should we choose to follow Jesus' example, we have to overcome the enemy in our own lives, just like He did in His. It means to die to self and become more and more like Jesus in what we say and do.

Sermons of Jesus Christ

⊠ Behavior ⊠ Jesus ⊠ Deliverance ⊠ Satan

Figure 6: Sermons of Jesus Christ

What was the gospel that Jesus taught? I completed a study on all the sermons of Jesus and found the following:

- 36% of Jesus' sermons centered on who He was and what His relationship with the Father and the Holy Spirit was. The people, and especially the Pharisees, often asked Jesus who He was. The people stood in amazement at the miracles and wonders He performed, while the Pharisees mostly saw Him as a threat. Jesus taught us through His sermons and His works about who He was. This was to help us to identify Him for who He was and is, but also to give us an example to imitate

- 31 % of Jesus' sermons taught people how to live in order to be blessed and not be cursed. The focus in these sermons was on human behavior. Jesus taught on what behavior is acceptable to God and what behavior will cause you to be cursed. Once you have chosen behavior that brings a curse over you the only way to deal with it effectively is through repentance and deliverance

- 11% of Jesus' sermons dealt with deliverance
- 22% of His sermons focused on who Satan and his demons are and provided us with information to identify their work in our lives.

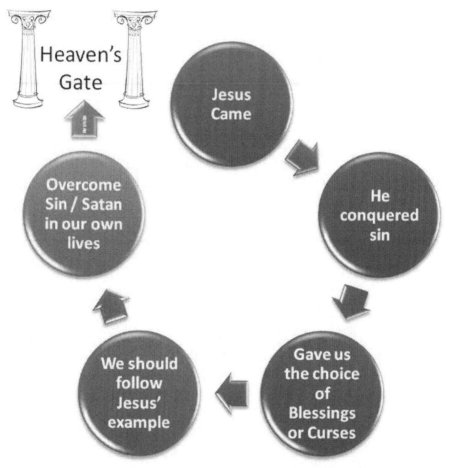

Figure 7: Jesus came to show us how to overcome

In summary the Gospel that Jesus preached is this:
- 1/3 of the time He gave us information on who He was and His reason for coming

- 1/3 of the time He taught us who we should become to be His followers and warned us that if we fail, we will be cursed and suffer punishment

- 1/3 of His teachings told us that we have an enemy that He has overcome and that we are to follow His example and overcome the enemy in our own lives

Healing the brokenhearted

The word "brokenhearted" refers to those people whose thoughts and/or feelings have been shattered or completely crushed. This gives us an idea of the power that Satan wields. The enemy will make you think that it's your own thoughts by placing them into your mind in the first person - for example, "I'm such a failure". Because the thought was placed in your mind in the first person, you automatically accept it as truth. This is a powerful way to launch an attack on an unsuspecting person. Not only can Satan and his demons shatter our thoughts but they can also break our hearts by crushing our feelings.

Our mind is one of Satan's favorite battlefields. He places negative thoughts into our minds and we accept them as our own thoughts. Once he's gotten us to accept these thoughts as our own, he proceeds to shatter and crush us. In Luke 12:29 Jesus teaches, "And do not seek what you should eat or what you should drink, nor have an anxious mind." We have to take our minds off earthly concerns and focus on Godly issues such as faith. Romans 12:2 says, "And do not be conformed to this world, but be transformed by the renewing of your mind, that you may prove what is that good and acceptable and perfect will of God." To renew your mind means to replace old thought patterns with new Godly ones. For example, if you fear the future, every time a fearful thought enters your mind you rebuke it and quote a scriptural principle or promise which will help you grow in faith – 2 Timothy 1:7, "For God has not given us a spirit of fear, but of power and of love and of a sound mind."

It is of the utmost importance to take note of every thought that enters your mind and not to entertain ungodly thoughts.

Feelings and actions stem from thoughts that you entertain in your mind. If Satan controls your thoughts, he also controls your feelings and your actions. Satan is the master of destruction. He will shatter your thoughts and crush your feelings if you do not submit your mind to God and constantly guard your thoughts.

As thoughts of fear, anxiety and stress usually lead to physical illness, there are certain thoughts that promote emotional brokenness. Thoughts of rejection, self-rejection and fear of rejection spiral into more negative thoughts of hatred, jealousy and acts of lust; all of these contribute toward emotional brokenness.

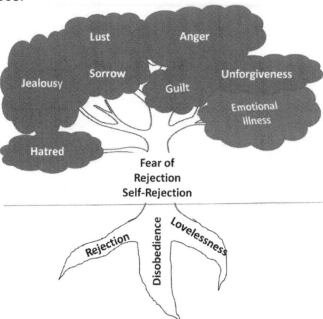

Figure 8: Roots of Emotional Brokenness

The path to emotional healing starts in your mind. You need to replace the negative thoughts you have entertained, with Godly thoughts. The most effective way to do this is to identify the lie that you accepted as the truth. Identify the first time you can remember where you accepted the lie Satan told you. In your mind's eye you should be able to remember clear details of what happened. Now prayerfully bring the episode before God and ask Him to show you where He was in that episode. God is omnipresent; therefore He was there when you got hurt. You need to find out what God actually wanted to teach you in that episode, instead of the lie Satan convinced you to believe. I'd like to share an example with you of how to apply this process. This will give you a clear demonstration of obtaining emotional healing.

As a little girl my mother once told me to make pancakes for my brother. My brother, who was two years older than I, was perfectly capable of making his own pancakes, but within our culture, it was expected of women to serve men. This belief resulted in all kinds of twisted perceptions for me. I had come to believe that boys were worthier than girls and girls had to serve them. Therefore I perceived myself as less worthy and subsequently thought that my performance in life was not as important as my brother's.

I remember how painful these thoughts were. After all, everybody wants to be special and treated fairly. The enemy had discovered my vulnerability and attacked it repeatedly throughout my life. Satan is good at making a mountain out of a molehill. An innocent request to bake my brother's pancakes had escalated into inferiority, rejection, rebellion, and attacked the way I believed I was perceived by those in authority.

It was only after I became aware of my problem years later, that I realized I needed emotional healing. I set out to discover what good God intended for me to gain from what I experienced. I realized that I was suffering from emotional brokenness and needed to address it before healing would manifest. I first identified the incident that had occurred in my past where I was attacked with rejection. I then asked God to show me where He was when these attacks took place. In a very simple and direct way God showed me where He was in this situation and brought healing and forgiveness.

This is what God showed me. I saw myself in my mom's kitchen where I was supposed to bake pancakes for my brother. I saw a bright light filling the kitchen and then I saw Jesus at the stove baking pancakes. He brought a pancake to me and said that He had come to serve. He then told me that when I serve others I become like Him. I asked the Lord about my mother and the role she had played. I still needed healing in this area. I then saw the Lord presiding as a judge. He sat looking at a paper in front of Him when He turned to me and asked, "Would you like Me to judge her?" I answered, "No, Lord, because I love her" He then said, "I love her too and will not judge her if you don't want me too". What wisdom! He is worthy of our highest praises!

The King of kings, who was a man, made and served me pancakes and then did not judge my mom because I asked Him not to. That turned my eyes to the Lord and His grace, and away from me and my mom and our flaws. I'm so thankful that the Lord brought emotional healing in such a kind manner.

God is visual and loves to speak in visions, dreams and pictures. He has shared this ability with us, and most of us can clearly recall pictures of our past. Hurtful pictures of the past can only be healed by bringing Jesus into them. He was there all along, but we have failed to see Him or what He was doing. If you need emotional healing, you need to see where He was and what He was doing when you suffered a broken heart. By communing with God on such issues you will experience lasting healing and spiritual growth.

God expects us to grow in our knowledge of Him. If we fail to gain knowledge the ultimate penalty is death, as is clear from Hosea 4:6, "My people are destroyed for lack of knowledge. Because you have rejected knowledge, I also will reject you from being priest for Me". As for those who do not submit their minds to God, Romans 1:28 rings a clear warning, "And even as they did not like to retain God in their knowledge, God gave them over to a debased mind, to do those things which are not fitting". It is your responsibility to grow in knowledge of God.

Scripture warns us of the consequences of worshipping our own minds or intellect. Ephesians 4:17-19 says, "This I say, therefore, and testify in the Lord, that you should no longer walk as the rest of the Gentiles walk, in the futility of their mind, having their understanding darkened, being alienated from the life of God, because of the ignorance that is in them, because of the blindness of their heart; who, being past feeling, have given themselves over to lewdness, to work all uncleanness with greediness." Philippians 3:19 takes this a step further, "whose end is destruction, whose god is their belly, and whose glory is in their shame--who set their mind on earthly things."

Jesus said He came to heal the brokenhearted. Are there any scriptures in the Gospels that can give us examples of how He healed the brokenhearted? For this exercise, I went to the book of Matthew and found the following:

- Matthew 4:24, "Then His fame went throughout all Syria; and they brought to Him all sick people who were afflicted with various diseases and torments, and those who were demon-possessed, epileptics, and paralytics; and He healed them." Jesus not only healed the diseases, but also those who were in torment. Torment refers to those who are in anguish or brokenhearted.

This scripture shows that even those who were in torment, received immediate healing. Many who minister to the brokenhearted claim that it is a process that takes time, but this is not what this Scripture shows. There is not even one example where Jesus ministered to the same brokenhearted person for months at a time. The fact is that Satan and his demons are those who destroy lives and crush feelings. When the demon is addressed and cast out, the brokenhearted person can be healed. To get rid of the scars on the heart, emotional healing must take place; and it is here where the person needs to bring Jesus into the "pictures" or memories where the hurt occurred. The demons bring in the pain, but Jesus brings the healing.

- Jesus healed the brokenhearted by casting out demons. (Matthew 8:28-34)

- Jesus multiplied the healing of the brokenhearted by training his disciples and others to cast out demons and to spread the good news of the Gospel. (Matthew 10)

- Jesus encouraged those who already believed through the working of miracles and wonders. (Matthew 11:2-6)

59

- The healing of the brokenhearted was reinforced by teaching them how to live a Godly life and how to receive God's mercy. These teachings would have exposed the lies that Satan had planted in their minds and lifted the heavy burdens the people carried. (Matthew 9:13; 11:28-30)

- The healing of the brokenhearted was also reinforced by teaching them how to pray effectively. (Matthew 6:9-13)

- Jesus encouraged the brokenhearted with words. (Matthew 12:20)

Jesus used the casting out of demons, teaching, encouragement and effective prayer to heal the brokenhearted; He taught His disciples how to do this and He expects all of us to do it as well.

To proclaim liberty to the captives

To proclaim something means to make a public declaration. This is not something that can be done in your inner room, it is done in public. It is done in front of those who are bound in a loud, clear voice filled with authority. Jesus publicly declared freedom to those who were enslaved and imprisoned.

On order to understand the significance of what Jesus is doing here we have to understand why a person will be imprisoned. When someone commits a serious crime and breaks a law for which the penalty is imprisonment, they will be put in a cell and locked up. This will continue until the debt owed by this person is paid and they are deemed fit to be released back into society.

In the spiritual world it works the same way. When someone breaks God's laws, they are found guilty and Satan gains the right to imprison them. These people can expect to experience the following:
- Inability to overcome specific sins – addictions, greed, hatred, idolatry, etc.

- Inability to gain victory in certain areas of their lives – constantly living in poverty; constantly being plagued by ill health

- Inability to enter God's presence – feeling that their prayers hit the ceiling; feeling spiritually dead, drained or weak; powerless

- Lack of faith – inability to display the signs Jesus said we should display in Mark 16:17

When proclaiming liberty to the captives, Jesus is sharing with them the way out of these prison cells. Repentance is the key to the prison doors. He calls them to repent of their sins before God and to sin no more. He shows them mercy and love by forgiving their sins, canceling out their debt, and releasing them into a life of freedom. This freedom refers to the right to make decisions with regards to your own life, no longer being a slave to sin.

Recovery of sight to the blind

God is a God of color, light and beauty. He created everything for us to see and enjoy. When you are blind, you are robbed of experiencing God's creation to the full extent that He created it to be enjoyed. There are many examples in the Bible where you read about Jesus healing the blind. Even today, many of God's anointed children pray for the blind and see their eyesight totally restored.

One example where Jesus prayed for restoration of sight is particularly interesting. When we pray for people to receive healing and it doesn't manifest immediately, we should continue praying, just like Jesus did. In Mark 8:22-25 Jesus prayed twice before the man's sight was perfectly restored, "Then He came to Bethsaida; and they brought a blind man to Him, and begged Him to touch him. So He took the blind man by the hand and led him out of the town. And when He had spit on his eyes and put His hands on him, He asked him if he saw anything. And he looked up and said, "I see men like trees, walking." Then He put His hands on his eyes again and made him look up. And he was restored and saw everyone clearly."

Sin leads to spiritual blindness, deafness and a lack of understanding. In Romans 11:8 we see that due to sin, God allowed a spirit of stupor within the people, "...God has given them a spirit of stupor, eyes that they should not see and ears that they should not hear, to this very day." A spirit of stupor is a demonic spirit and can be cast out, once repentance has taken place. In this case the people sinned against God by rejecting Him and His prophets, and through idolatry – bowing their knees before Baal. God punished them by allowing a spirit of stupor to enter them and keep them from revelation and understanding spiritual issues.

Jesus also came to open the spiritual eyes and to bring understanding to those who have none. In Matthew 13:15-16 Jesus says, "For the hearts of this people have grown dull. Their ears are hard of hearing, and their eyes they have closed, lest they should see with their eyes and hear with their ears, lest they should understand with their hearts and turn, so that I should heal them."

What I find even more powerful is how many people were restored to God through Jesus' ministry. Jesus opened the eyes of the spiritually blind of those whom He was sent to turn to God. We see this in John 17:12, "While I was with them in the world, I kept them in Your name. Those whom You gave Me I have kept; and none of them is lost except the son of perdition, that the Scripture might be fulfilled."

It is clear from Biblical examples that our spiritual eyes can be closed and opened. In Luke 24:16 the two travelers to Emmaus did not recognize Jesus, "But their eyes were restrained, so that they did not know Him." Yet in Luke 24:31, their spiritual eyes were opened and they recognized Jesus, "Then their eyes were opened and they knew Him; and He vanished from their sight." When your spiritual eyes are opened it usually means that you have gained understanding and revelation. Understanding and revelation come only through the Spirit of God; therefore, if you have not been baptized with the Holy Spirit, you will not understand the things of God.

In Acts 26:18 Jesus commissions Paul, saying, "...to open their eyes, in order to turn them from darkness to light, and from the power of Satan to God, that they may receive forgiveness of sins and an inheritance among those who are sanctified by faith in Me." This commission is one that each one of us should take as our own. Just as Jesus opened our spiritual eyes, we should do the same for others through the work of the Holy Spirit within us. We should turn others from the power of Satan to God, help them to identify the sin in their lives and have them repent of their sins. We should pray prayers of deliverance with them, casting out demons and ripping them out of the prisons of the enemy. We should pray with them to be filled with the Holy Spirit so that they may receive revelation and understanding and that their spiritual eyes may be opened.

In Hebrew 5:14 we are given keys to obtain spiritual maturity, "But solid food belongs to those who are of full age, that is, those who by reason of use have their senses exercised to discern both good and evil." This scripture encourages us to regularly use our senses to discern good and evil. Our senses include our eyesight, hearing, smell, taste and feelings; all of these must regularly be used to tell the difference between what is good and evil. Jesus came to restore our sight but it is up to us to exercise our senses and use them to remain on the right path, and help others to do the same.

To set at liberty those who are oppressed

Jesus makes a distinction between captivity and oppression. Captivity is addressed by means of a declaration, whereas oppression requires an action to take place – "...to set at...". Through this work Jesus changes the circumstances of a person from one who is held down, being dominated and afflicted, to one who is free. This is more than a declaration; it is an action which moves a person from a place of immobility to mobility. When you are delivered by Jesus, your rights to rule over the earth have been restored. It is however, up to you to take up the reins and not to continue living in defeat.

What opens the door for oppression in your life? In Deuteronomy 28:15 we read, "But it shall come to pass, if you do not obey the voice of the LORD your God, to observe carefully all His commandments and His statutes which I command you today, that all these curses will come upon you and overtake you:" A few verses later, in Deuteronomy 28:29, oppression is mentioned as one of the curses that comes upon you, "And you shall grope at noonday, as a blind man gropes in darkness; you shall not prosper in your ways; you shall be only oppressed and plundered continually, and no one shall save you." Deuteronomy 28:33 reveals another curse of oppression which will be unleashed upon you for not observing God's commandments, "A nation whom you have not known shall eat the fruit of your land and the produce of your labor, and you shall be only oppressed and crushed continually." Being oppressed is similar to being in slavery.

Do you recognize the fruits of these curses in your life? If so, do you want to be set free by the Lord? It's really easy to do because Jesus has already paid the price; we only need to apply the solution He provided. Start by repenting for not observing God's commandments. When we cry out to God in our time of oppression, He hears every cry and He pities us. Judges 2:18 confirms this, "...for the LORD was moved to pity by their groaning because of those who oppressed them and harassed them." God was so moved by their groaning that He raised up judges for them and delivered them out of the hand of their enemies all the days of the judges. God then raised up a Savior, Jesus, for us – He is the ultimate Judge and we are delivered by Him!

God wants to do more than just deliver us, He also wants to give us the land of our enemies. In Judges 6:9 we see God's heart regarding His children who are oppressed, "and I delivered you out of the hand of the Egyptians and out of the hand of all who oppressed you, and drove them out before you and gave you their land." God is the only One who may judge and His judgment overrides all others. Psalm 103:6 promises us that God will see to it that justice is done, "The LORD executes righteousness And justice for all who are oppressed."

Get to know the commandments and observe them carefully. Ask the Lord to lift these curses from you and to teach you by His Spirit and to bless you and your children.

To proclaim the acceptable year of the Lord

Here we see Jesus making another public proclamation that the acceptable year of the Lord has arrived; it is here! At last the relationship between God and mankind has been restored and man's debt to God has been settled. Somebody paid a price that was found acceptable by the Father! That Somebody was Jesus Christ.

So what is it about God's creation that He found unacceptable up to now? Adam sinned; he failed to obey God's commandments. I am a parent and realize that the Father was angered by the display of lovelessness and disrespect more than the failure to obey His commands. Before Adam fell in sin, there was a love relationship and hardly any rules or laws. Sin necessitated the establishment of the commandments. Unfortunately, amongst men not even one found who could obey all the commandments. God had to find another way for man to pay his debt and for this love relationship to be restored.

Instead of punishing man with death, God made a way by sending His own Son to pay Adam's debt (mankind's debt). A new covenant was made between God and man – one which allows us to ask forgiveness when we sin, instead of dying because of it. This new covenant no longer relies on mankind's willpower to remain righteous, but it brings man to a place where he knows that he needs God within him to be victorious over sin. We serve a loving God; one who loves to display His love and mercy. Our God is confident enough about the power of true love that He put a new commandment in place based on love between Him and mankind, and called it "the acceptable year of the Lord".

Jesus proclaimed this new way that God has made for us to restore our relationship with the Father. It does not happen automatically nor covers the whole of humanity – it covers only those who enter into a covenant relationship with Jesus. He is the One who paid the price and He is the One who applies His own blood to wash away our debt before the Father.

Acts 2:38 says, "Then Peter said to them, "Repent, and let every one of you be baptized in the name of Jesus Christ for the remission of sins; and you shall receive the gift of the Holy Spirit." In Mark 12:33 it emphasizes the importance of the new covenant, "And to love Him with all the heart, with all the understanding, with all the soul, and with all the strength, and to love one's neighbor as oneself, is more than all the whole burnt offerings and sacrifices."

What a wonderful privilege it is to live in a time when "the acceptable year of the Lord" has already been proclaimed! With this privilege comes an enormous responsibility. Let's not shun this price that Jesus paid for our freedom and continue to live under the oppressive yoke of the enemy. Have the guts to believe Jesus and to become just like Him. Your love relationship with the Father has been restored. Your position of rulership has been restored. Take it up, reign with Jesus in heavenly places and let the power of Satan be under your feet.

CHAPTER FOUR

They will cast out demons

Introduction

To follow Jesus certainly requires faith. How wild is this? Jesus expects of us to cast out demons when most of us can't even see them. And as if that is not a big enough step in faith, He adds weight to this command by saying that the casting out of demons will be one of the ways by which to identify those who follow Him. This should elevate the casting out of demons to a really high priority in every Christians' life. To cast out demons goes beyond faith in Jesus, it requires you to act in faith. To make it even more interesting, when you cast out demons you are no longer operating in the Lord's "friendly zone", you actually encounter opposition and attack from Satan and his demons. You take your first steps out of the "demilitarized zone" and onto a battlefield where your enemy sees all your weaknesses and you have to walk in faith!

The picture I have painted is not a rosy one. By acting in faith you find yourself on a battlefield. You have demons opposing you; you have a lack of knowledge and barriers of people you minister to, that you have to bear in mind. You often have the church leadership opposing you and you have to work on keeping up your own level of faith. On the other hand, you have the Lord's requirement and the desperate need you come across in those you minister to, motivating you to act in faith. The real breakthrough comes when you see God act on your behalf and deliver the dying and the hopeless and He brings immediate restoration to them. You will never be the same after such an experience – it is spiritually addictive! You will know that you are safe in God's hands; you will know that He is the "Man of War" and will never forsake you; you will know that you, and those you minister to, have a soft place to fall and that no sin is too big that it brings permanent separation between you and God.

The Lord entrusted the keys of Heaven to the church, and in particular, to the leadership of the church. The keys are the authority given by Jesus to bind and loose on earth and in the heavens. Jesus expects His church to move past the basics of Christianity and into the Spirit filled walk of holiness. If you are in a leadership position in the church, you need to find this path of holiness and share it with those the Lord has placed in your care.

"They will cast out demons" is the first sign Jesus mentioned. I believe there is a good reason why it was mentioned first – I believe it is a very important sign to display. Mark 16:15-19 basically describes the summary of Jesus' final command to His followers, before His ascension. To cast out demons is the first sign mentioned by Jesus.

Deliverance often precedes physical or emotional healing, as can be seen in Luke 4:39-41, "So He stood over her and rebuked the fever, and it left her. And immediately she arose and served them. When the sun was setting, all those who had any that were sick with various diseases brought them to Him; and He laid His hands on every one of them and healed them. And demons also came out of many…" Deliverance is God in action and it's an opportunity to witness God's awesome power at work. This gives us confidence to take up serpents or fight demons; it stirs up our faith in the protection we enjoy in the Lord. Deliverance involves the body of Christ working together to serve one another, and at the same time, seeing the manifest power of God in action.

Your spiritual growth advances according to the measure in which you attain victory over demonic forces in your own life. Deliverance is a daily part of your walk on the path of holiness. Solomon shares some of his wisdom with us about the path we choose to walk in Proverbs 4:14, 26-27 by saying, "Do not enter the path of the wicked, and do not walk in the way of evil. Ponder the path of your feet, and let all your ways be established. Do not turn to the right or the left; remove your foot from evil." Deliverance is also instrumental in receiving the gift of tongues. Heartfelt confession and repentance of sins and the casting out of demons cleanses a person and allows a greater flow of the Holy Spirit within. Deliverance brings great joy and glory to God. Luke 10:21 says, "In that hour Jesus rejoiced in the Spirit…"

71

Deliverance signifies man actively taking up the God-given task of rulership over sin. In Ephesians 1:20-21, it clearly states Christ's rulership over Satan's kingdom, "which He worked in Christ when He raised Him from the dead and seated Him at His right hand in the heavenly places, far above all principality and power and might and dominion, and every name that is named, not only in this age but also in that which is to come". When we this a step further, Ephesians 2:6 shows our current place of rulership through Jesus Christ, "and raised us up together, and made us sit together in the heavenly places in Christ Jesus". In deliverance you therefore see man facing his enemy with full confidence, faith and trust in the power available to him through Jesus Christ.

A strong personal unity and love relationship exists between a person in the deliverance ministry, and God. A person who ministers deliverance must be filled with the Holy Spirit, because it is the Spirit of God that operates through the deliverance minister that has the authority to cast out demons. The use of Jesus' name without the reinforcement of God's power through the Holy Spirit, will anger the demons, and such a person attempting deliverance will be attacked by the demons.

In order to be identified as a follower of Jesus, we have to follow His example. What was the example that Jesus gave us with regard to deliverance? The book of Luke points out 49 different occasions on which Jesus teaches about Satan and his demons. Jesus talks more about Satan and his demons and how to overcome them, than the number of times he teaches on how to walk on the path of holiness. Let's take some time and examine Jesus in action when He cast out demons. Examining Biblical examples ensures clarification on any controversial issues that might arise when discussing deliverance.

Jesus casts out an unclean spirit in the synagogue

Luke 4:33-36, "Now in the synagogue there was a man who had a spirit of an unclean demon. And he cried out with a loud voice, saying, "Let us alone! What have we to do with You, Jesus of Nazareth? Did

You come to destroy us? I know who You are--the Holy One of God!" But Jesus rebuked him, saying, "Be quiet, and come out of him!" And when the demon had thrown him in their midst, it came out of him and did not hurt him. Then they were all amazed and spoke among themselves, saying, "What a word this is! For with authority and power He commands the unclean spirits, and they come out."

This example shows that Jesus cast the demon out in the synagogue. It stands to reason that this man was a member of the synagogue and believed in God. Not only did this man have an unclean spirit living inside of him, but this demon manifested by speaking through the man. Demons live in the spiritual realm and it's easy for them to identify the authority of Jesus as the Son of God. Jesus does not want acknowledgement from demonic spirits and commands them to be quiet.

What can we learn from this example?

- Church-going Christians can have demons

   We often come across Christians who deny that they can have demons. Let's look at what the Bible has to say about this. On two occasions Jesus identified evil entities at work in His own disciples: John 6:70-71, "Jesus answered them, "Did I not choose you, the twelve and one of you is a devil?" He spoke of Judas Iscariot, the son of Simon, for it was he who would betray Him, being one of the twelve." Luke 9:54-55, "And when His disciples James and John saw this, they said, "Lord, do You want us to command fire to come down from heaven and consume them, just as Elijah did?" But He turned and rebuked them, and said, "You do not know what manner of spirit you are of." The fact is: Christians can have demons!

- Demons can speak through people

- Demons recognize and acknowledge the Lord

- Demons know that the Lord has power over them, that's why they wanted to know if Jesus came to destroy them

73

- Jesus did not want any affirmation or acknowledgement from the demons – neither should we. Jesus talked to Satan and he talked to demons but He did not want them to verify who He was. We should do the same. We do not seek verification from demons; nor do we enter into conversations with them. Besides, they work for the master of deception and lies, and tend to have the same characteristics

- Demons have to obey a command from God. They left the man when Jesus commanded them to leave

- Demons usually manifest when they leave a person. In this case they threw the man before leaving him

- The demons did not hurt the man, even though they had thrown him down

- The people were amazed at what they saw and talked among themselves. Jesus did the deliverance in the synagogue amongst the people. They all witnessed the deliverance and recognized the authority and power that was displayed when the demons were cast out. Why is it that most church leaders today don't allow deliverances to take place in their churches? Surely if Jesus gave us this example, it is perfect? Could it be that those church leaders, who forbid deliverances to take place in their churches, have established their own rules that differ from God's example? It is these leaders that are robbing the members of their congregations of the opportunity of seeing the power of God in operation, thereby condemning their flocks to live lives of defeat at the hand of Satan and his demons

Jesus casts out a demon of fever

Luke 4:38-39, "Now He arose from the synagogue and entered Simon's house. But Simon's wife's mother was sick with a high fever, and they made request of Him concerning her. So He stood over her and rebuked the fever, and it left her. And immediately she arose and served them."

74

What can we learn from this example?

- Fever is a demon and it can be rebuked. This means that illness is caused by demons, can be cast out and healing can be obtained immediately

- It is well known that fever is usually caused by an infection or inflammation in the body. The word infection has a very apt description and implies that a contagion has entered the body. In the spiritual world the contagion is usually a demon of fear, anxiety or stress. These demons gain entrance because the person has entertained such thoughts instead of rebuking them and walking in faith.

  Your spiritual body is a lot like your physical body. If you take care of your physical body by regularly feeding it good nutritious food, drinking plenty of water and exercising regularly, it will usually be in good shape. If a person's spirit is not regularly fed nutritious food, well protected and washed and kept alive with the rivers of living water that flow from God's throne, your spiritual body will not be in good shape and will be unable to withstand demonic attacks. If thoughts of fear, anxiety or stress are regularly entertained, demons will enter. These demons act as contagions of your spirit person and soon, just like in the case of an apple with a worm, your whole body and spirit will become rotten.

- The sick woman did not ask for deliverance, instead those who loved her requested it on her behalf. Jesus honored their request and she was healed. Sick people are often too drained to act on their own behalf. It's important to surround yourself with others who are strong in faith. In a time of need, these people will be there to pray with you and support you

- Jesus rebuked the fever. Once again it is clear that Jesus spoke to the demon. Demons are cast out by speaking with the authority that God endowed us with and it is done in the name of Jesus Christ who came in the flesh

- The woman was immediately healed. Deliverance usually results in immediate healing

Jesus cast demons out of many

Luke 4:40-41, "When the sun was setting, all those who had any that were sick with various diseases brought them to Him; and He laid His hands on every one of them and healed them. And demons also came out of many, crying out and saying, "You are the Christ, the Son of God!" And He, rebuking them, did not allow them to speak, for they knew that He was the Christ."

What can we learn from this example?
- Healing the sick and driving out demons draws crowds of people
- Various diseases are healed by the laying on of hands and casting out of demons
- The demons spoke through the people
- The demons acknowledged Jesus' authority and His standing as God's Son
- Jesus did not allow the demons to speak because they were testifying to who He was
- The people were immediately healed from various diseases
- In this case Jesus ministered to everyone of those who were brought to Him for ministry

Jesus forgives a paralyzed man's sins

Luke 5:17-21, "Now it happened on a certain day, as He was teaching, that there were Pharisees and teachers of the law sitting by, who had come out of every town of Galilee, Judea, and Jerusalem. And the power of the Lord was present to heal them. Then behold, men brought on a bed a man who was paralyzed, whom they sought to bring in and lay before Him. And when they could not find how they might bring him in, because of the crowd, they went up on the housetop and let him down with his bed through the tiling into the midst before Jesus. When He saw their faith, He said to him, "Man, your sins are forgiven you." And the scribes and the Pharisees began to reason, saying, "Who is this who speaks blasphemies? Who can forgive sins but God alone?"".

What can we learn from this example?

- Today's church leadership also gathers to observe, learn from and reason about the work of God. The Pharisees lived and judged others according to their own interpretation of Biblical laws. Church leaders often stem the flow of the Holy Spirit by implementing laws according to their own interpretation in their churches. We are called to be led by the Holy Spirit and not blocked by man-made rules that oppose the work of the Lord. The church leadership has a responsibility to constantly test the laws within their congregations to make sure they are not put in place to protect their own interests, fears or insecurities

- The Pharisees failed to recognize the Lord and called His work "Blasphemies". The same still happens to those who do deliverance today. They are criticized and blocked from doing God's work by church leaders who would rather criticize Christ than follow Him in Spirit and truth

- Crowds of people gather where the power of God is present and healing and deliverance take place

- Friends helped the man, who could not help himself into the presence of the Lord

- The Lord rewards and approves of faith in Him. The faith that these men showed by not stopping at any obstacles in helping their friend to be ministered to by Jesus, pleased Him and He reacted by meeting their need. If you have a friend in need, show your love for him/her by bringing them in faith before the Lord. A display of our faith in the Lord often precedes the power of the Lord in operation

- Jesus spoke forgiveness over the man. It is important to ask forgiveness for sins, but it is equally important to accept the forgiveness. I firmly believe that the inability of people to receive forgiveness keeps them in a state of torment and illness. A crucial part of deliverance is repentance of sin and asking God for forgiveness. God says that if we repent, He will forgive us. We should do likewise. Jesus taught his disciples how to cast out demons and then sent them out to do it. In Mark 6:12-13 it says, "So they went out and preached that people should repent. And they cast out many demons, and anointed with oil many who were sick, and healed them." It is very interesting to note that the disciples first preached that people should repent – without repentance no deliverance can take place!

Jesus casts Legion out of a man living amongst the tombs

Luke 8:27-39, "And when He stepped out on the land, there met Him a certain man from the city who had demons for a long time. And he wore no clothes, nor did he live in a house but in the tombs. When he saw Jesus, he cried out, fell down before Him, and with a loud voice said, "What have I to do with You, Jesus, Son of the Most High God? I beg You, do not torment me!" For He had commanded the unclean spirit to come out of the man.

For it had often seized him, and he was kept under guard, bound with chains and shackles; and he broke the bonds and was driven by the demon into the wilderness. Jesus asked him, saying, "What is your name?" And he said, "Legion," because many demons had entered him. And they begged Him that He would not command them to go out into the abyss.

Now a herd of many swine was feeding there on the mountain. So they begged Him that He would permit them to enter them. And He

78

permitted them. Then the demons went out of the man and entered the swine, and the herd ran violently down the steep place into the lake and drowned. When those who fed them saw what had happened, they fled and told it in the city and in the country. Then they went out to see what had happened, and came to Jesus, and found the man from whom the demons had departed, sitting at the feet of Jesus, clothed and in his right mind. And they were afraid. They also who had seen it told them by what means he who had been demon-possessed was healed.

Then the whole multitude of the surrounding region of the Gadarenes asked Him to depart from them, for they were seized with great fear. And He got into the boat and returned. Now the man from whom the demons had departed begged Him that he might be with Him. But Jesus sent him away, saying, "Return to your own house, and tell what great things God has done for you." And he went his way and proclaimed throughout the whole city what great things Jesus had done for him."

What can we learn from this example?

- Long-term and severe demon infestation leads to possession. This man was infested with demons for a long time. If a demon is allowed into your life and left unchallenged, it will eventually possess you. Possession means that you have handed over all rights you have to the demons and they control you

- The demon-possessed are supernaturally strong. This man was a danger to him and to others and had to be guarded and kept in chains and shackles. The demons managed to break him free and forced him to live in filth, naked amongst the tombs. It is surprising how accurately your physical situation reflects your spiritual situation. This man was naked in the flesh and in a state of total exposure to the demonic in the spiritual. He was living in filth in the flesh and living under demon control in the spirit. He was living amongst those already dead in the physical and the spiritual realms. He lost all control over himself in the physical and in the spiritual

79

- Demons speak through the demon possessed. The demons acknowledged Jesus as the Son of the Most High God. The demons knelt before Jesus and begged Him not to torment them, thereby acknowledging that Jesus had the power and the right to do so. They also asked permission to enter the pigs

- Demons have to obey Jesus' command. The demons begged Him to give a command for them to enter the pigs, thereby acknowledging that Jesus had the right to command them and that they had to obey Him

- The demons have meaningful names. Jesus asked the demon who he was and the demon said his name was "Legion". The meaning of Legion is that it indicated the largest unit in the Roman army consisting of 3000 to 6000 soldiers. This man was infested by many demons. If Jesus found it necessary to identify His enemy before dealing with it, shouldn't we? The truth is that the names of the demons tell us more about who they are. It is much easier to deal with an enemy you know than one you don't; especially if you take into consideration that your enemy has been around since the beginning of the earth and probably knows you better than you know yourself

Michael and I have written a book on the satanic principalities and powers that will provide you with valuable information about your spiritual enemies. The name of the book is "Who Are You" and is available from Amazon.com, Xulon Press and on order from any bookstore. This book will show you what the Bible has to say about this evil army; how to identify its attacks in your life and will equip you to effectively overcome it. It will reveal to you the hierarchy of the enemy with details of the rankings and names. You will be made aware of biblical knowledge that Satan has hidden in plain sight for the sole purpose of keeping you from walking in God's blessings and protection. This book will challenge you to evaluate your own walk with God, exposing the work of the enemy in your life and highlighting opportunities for growth, to enhance your walk with the Lord

- Demons' work is to kill, steal and destroy. The demons in this man stole his life and his right to make choices. He lost everything, even his own life. These demons were terrified that Jesus would condemn them to the abyss, which is the place reserved for them after Jesus' second coming. Jesus allowed the demons to enter the pigs and kill them all. These demons that had destroyed the man's life, killed the pigs and robbed the people in the area of the income they would have derived from their livestock

- People tend to value their financial wellbeing more than the deliverance and healing of an individual. Jesus allowed them to enter the pigs because their time had not yet arrived to go to the abyss. Instead the demons served as a further test for the people who lived in the region. These people derived income from their livestock and the loss of a herd had a severe impact on their financial wellbeing. The people asked Jesus to leave because of this loss. This tendency is prevalent in people today. Many church leaders won't allow deliverance in their churches because they fear that those who attend the church will object, leave and that their own personal income will then dwindle or dry up altogether

- The demon possessed man was totally healed. This man begged Jesus to allow him to remain with Him, but Jesus encouraged him to go home, glorify God and share his testimony with others. Deliverance is effective in healing demon possession and restoring people to a normal life. What a powerful testimony this man had. Demon possession should also be viewed as a great opportunity for deliverance and a powerful testimony to the glory of God

Jesus rebukes the wind and raging water

Luke 8:24-25, "And they came to Him and awoke Him, saying, "Master, Master, we are perishing!" Then He arose and rebuked the wind and the raging of the water. And they ceased, and there was a calm. But He said to them, "Where is your faith?" And they were afraid, and marveled, saying to one another, "Who can this be? For He commands even the winds and water, and they obey Him!"''

What can we learn from this example?

- In spiritual warfare, Satan will use all that he can, even the physical elements here on earth. Our warfare will at times be directed to address demons operating through the wind, water, earth or fire to cause destruction or death. Once you step out of the man-made boundaries you've placed God in, you enter the realm of mighty miracles! On several occasions, I have personally rebuked thunderstorms and raging fires and have seen them cease immediately. You have to exercise your faith in God and realize that the Spirit of God speaks with the same creative power that spoke the universe into being; the same Spirit that is in those who believe

- Jesus spoke words of rebuke to the wind and the raging water and it immediately obeyed and calmed down

- Jesus expects us to have faith and to take authority over demonic attacks, even the ones launched using the elements

Jesus heals a woman with blood flow

Mark 5:24-34, "So Jesus went with him, and a great multitude followed Him and thronged Him. Now a certain woman had a flow of blood for twelve years, and had suffered many things from many physicians. She had spent all that she had and was no better, but rather grew worse.

When she heard about Jesus, she came behind Him in the crowd and touched His garment. For she said, "If only I may touch His clothes, I shall be made well." Immediately the fountain of her blood was dried up, and she felt in her body that she was healed of the affliction. And Jesus, immediately knowing in Himself that power had gone out of Him, turned around in the crowd and said, "Who touched My clothes?" But His disciples said to Him, "You see the multitude thronging You, and You say, 'Who touched Me?' "

And He looked around to see her who had done this thing. But the woman, fearing and trembling, knowing what had happened to her, came and fell down before Him and told Him the whole truth. And He said to her, "Daughter, your faith has made you well. Go in peace, and be healed of your affliction."

What can we learn from this example?

- A high level of faith in Jesus can affect deliverance. Jesus doesn't have to audibly speak deliverance to us. If our faith in Him is strong enough we only need to spend time in His presence, touching Him and we will experience His deliverance – just as the woman who touched his garment and was healed.

  This kind of deliverance is especially prevalent when large groups of people are gathered together. The corporate level of faith rises and the power of the Lord overcomes the people and works the deliverance without any specific words having to be spoken.

  Although many may disagree, group deliverance is scriptural. There are several examples where Jesus ministered to groups of people and all of them were healed and delivered. We are also subject to deliverance when we are constantly washed by the Word of God. An example of this can be seen in John 13:8-11, "Peter said to Him, "You shall never wash my feet!" Jesus answered him, "If I do not wash you, you have no part with Me." Simon Peter said to Him, "Lord, not my feet only, but also my hands and my head!" Jesus said to him, "He who is bathed needs only to wash his feet, but is completely clean; and you are clean, but not all of you." For He knew who would betray Him; therefore He said, "You are not all clean.""

  I believe that Jesus is referring to the importance of being washed by the Word of God and experiencing deliverance. The disciples were with Jesus most of the time and they were constantly being washed by the words that He spoke. It's interesting to note that Jesus said that only their feet needed to be cleaned. Spiritually, your feet are the part of your spirit person that connects with the physical world. As we walk and interact in the physical world, the feet of our spirit person become dirty. I believe that this is the reason that Jesus washed their feet – it was a symbolic gesture that we need to help each other keep clean from the influences of the world. Jesus spoke of Judas as the one not being clean, because He knew that Judas had already accepted what the physical world had to offer and would therefore betray Him

- Deliverance is done by Jesus' power. Jesus perceived power going out from Him as the woman touched his garment. This is a wonderful example of deliverance that takes place because of strong faith in the healing ability of Jesus. The woman was immediately healed of her affliction

- People are more important to Jesus than laws. According to law this woman was considered unclean and was not allowed to touch the Lord, or any man, while she was experiencing blood flow. The Lord was more concerned about her wellbeing and spoke words of peace and healing to her instead of condemnation. We serve a God of mercy who is quick to demonstrate His love. Jesus came to bring us a new covenant, one based on mercy and love

- Demons rob you of your health and finances. The woman was ill for 12 years and spent all her finances on trying to find a cure. How is it that this still goes on today when we can turn to the Lord who will give freely to those who believe?

Jesus casts a demon out of a mute man

Matthew 9:32-34, "As they went out, behold, they brought to Him a man, mute and demon-possessed. And when the demon was cast out, the mute spoke. And the multitudes marveled, saying, "It was never seen like this in Israel!" But the Pharisees said, "He casts out demons by the ruler of the demons.""

What can we learn from this example?

- Demons cause muteness and when cast out by the Lord, the mute will speak

- People marvel when they see the deliverance and healings that Jesus brings

- The church leadership said that the demons were cast out by the authority of Satan. Even today, many church leaders don't know Jesus personally and fear deliverance because it can only be understood and performed when you are filled with the Holy Spirit

Jesus casts demons out of an epileptic boy

Luke 9:38-43, "Suddenly a man from the multitude cried out, saying, "Teacher, I implore You, look on my son, for he is my only child. And behold, a spirit seizes him, and he suddenly cries out; it convulses him so that he foams at the mouth; and it departs from him with great difficulty, bruising him. So I implored Your disciples to cast it out, but they could not."

Then Jesus answered and said, "O faithless and perverse generation, how long shall I be with you and bear with you? Bring your son here." And as he was still coming, the demon threw him down and convulsed him. Then Jesus rebuked the unclean spirit, healed the child, and gave him back to his father. And they were all amazed at the majesty of God. But while everyone marveled at all the things which Jesus did..."

What can we learn from this example?

- People without faith will not be successful in all deliverances. It is of the utmost importance to have faith in God when you minister deliverance. The level of faith needed will depend on the ranking of the demons you are dealing with and the level of infestation you will be facing

- People who are perverse will not be successful in all deliverances. Jesus gave clues as to why His disciples were unable to cast the demons out. The first was that they lacked faith and the second was perversity. The root word for "perverse" is to "turn away" – this implies that the disciples were taught how to cast out demons but turned away from what they were taught. Perverse also means "corrupt" which indicates that the disciples were not pure but still had sins that they were dealing with. It is important to realize that deliverance is God's work and to keep your eyes, trust, hope and expectation focused on God and not on the enemy or the people around you. We all sin and fall short of the glory of God, but still God chooses to work through us. His power and anointing will do the work – therefore ALL honor and glory goes to God!

- Demons enter and torment children. Satan and his demons will not have mercy on children. They enjoy targeting all children with fear. Most children still have the ability to easily see into the spirit realm. Demons know this and like to terrorize them with terrifying images at times when they are alone or sleeping. In these circumstances, children will complain of being scared and seeing monsters or scary things in their rooms at night. Never disregard or make light of the situation when your child comes to you to tell you of these things. Get active; search their rooms for ungodly toys, games, movies, books, etc. We have found that most of the toys given out by fast-food chains are not innocent. Destroy any items you find that you feel convicted about, and ask God to forgive you for allowing these objects into your house. Bind the spirit of fear and terror in your child and cast it out in a soft, authoritative manner when your child is already asleep. Remember to clothe yourself and your family members with the armor of God as described in Ephesians 6, and ask God to send His angels to protect you and your loved ones.

Many years ago I ministered to a little boy about 7 years old. His mother had told us that he was so terrified at night that he couldn't sleep and that he refused to be in his room by himself. The fear robbed him of sleep and it was having a negative effect on his school work. The teachers let his mother know that he would probably have to repeat his current grade because his results were so poor.

We had to minister very gently to the boy and we allowed him to sit on his mother's lap during the whole deliverance session. One after another we bound and cast out the demons that tormented the boy. Shortly thereafter, the mother reported that her son had been able to sleep well and remarkable improvement in her son's behavior had followed. Two months later she let us know that her son had made a complete turnaround at school. By the end of the school year, the little boy had not only passed his yearly exams, but had actually ranked first in his class! How wonderful is the God we serve!

You might ask what rights Satan and his demons have to attack your children. In Deuteronomy 5:9 it says, "...you shall not bow down to them nor serve them. For I, the LORD your God, am a jealous God, visiting the iniquity of the fathers upon the children to the third and fourth generations of those who hate Me..." Idolatry by your ancestors will provide an open door for demons to attack you and your children. If the idolatry is not confessed as a sin and repented of before God, He will not intervene on your behalf to bring deliverance.

- Demon manifestations can be seen, heard and felt. The demons in this example caused the boy to cry out; they convulsed him so that he foamed at the mouth; and they departed from him with great difficulty, bruising him. Demons that cause physically illness usually manifest physically, often causing pain, before being cast out. On the other hand, demons that cause emotional problems seem to manifest more emotionally when they are cast out. Demons that attack the mind usually cause dizziness, confusion or hearing of demonic voices before being cast out. Spirits of Satanism or witchcraft will act rebellious, confrontational, cause the person to experience great fear, dizziness; they will shout out profanities, show ungodly signs and cause foul smelling odors to permeate the air

Jesus gave His disciples authority over all demons

Luke 9:1-2: "Then He called His twelve disciples together and gave them power and authority over all demons, and to cure diseases. He sent them to preach the kingdom of God and to heal the sick."

What can we learn from this example?

- Jesus has authority and power over all demons. Some people think that Jesus only received power and authority over all demons when He died on the cross, but this is not the case. You cannot rightfully give something away if it didn't already belong to you. Jesus empowered His disciples to cast out demons before His crucifixion

- Jesus' disciples received His authority and power over all demons. Here we see Jesus giving authority and power over all demons to His disciples and then sending them out to preach the kingdom of God and to heal the sick

Jesus approved of others casting out demons in His name

Luke 9:49-50, "Now John answered and said, "Master, we saw someone casting out demons in Your name, and we forbade him because he does not follow with us." But Jesus said to him, "Do not forbid him, for he who is not against us is on our side.""

What can we learn from this example?

- There will be others who are not part of your immediate circle of acquaintances who will also be walking in the signs of Jesus and it is not our place to stop them

Jesus empowers 70 others to cast out demons

Luke 10:17-19, "Then the seventy returned with joy, saying, "Lord, even the demons are subject to us in Your name." And He said to them, "I saw Satan fall like lightning from heaven. Behold, I give you the authority to trample on serpents and scorpions, and over all the power of the enemy, and nothing shall by any means hurt you."

What can we learn from this example?

- The name of Jesus is used to cast out demons. This is a key to successful deliverance. When you minister deliverance you are entering the Father's presence clothed in the righteousness of Christ. If you do it in your own righteousness you will fail because you still have sin in your own life that you are working through. You have to be fully aware that you are only the vessel that the Father has chosen to work through, and that nothing good that comes out of deliverance has anything to do with you. You are doing it in Jesus' name, His authority and His power. In itself, it is a great honor and privilege to be used by God in such a way, and the benefits you reap are being able to see the power of God in action, have your faith level raised and see the magnitude of God's mercy and love for us. It stands to reason that all glory and thanksgiving goes to God alone!

- We receive Jesus' authority and power to cast out demons. Jesus gives us the authority to trample on serpents and scorpions, and over all the power of the enemy. Demons have to obey a Spirit-filled child of God when they use the name of Jesus to cast them out. A reason why deliverance does not always work is found in our own failings, not in God failing us

- Nothing shall by any means hurt you. When you are sent by God to cast out demons, nothing will by any means hurt you. You are under the protection of the Creator and sustainer of life who has already overcome the enemy. It is God's wish for us to overcome the enemy in our own lives and that we should rule over sin, because Jesus made a way for us to do so. Satan's mission is to steal, kill and destroy, but when we become more like Jesus, we will walk in divine protection and grace

Knowledge of deliverance is hidden from the wise and prudent

Luke 10:21, "In that hour Jesus rejoiced in the Spirit and said, "I thank You, Father, Lord of heaven and earth, that You have hidden these things from the wise and prudent and revealed them to babes."

What can we learn from this scripture?
- Jesus rejoiced when He saw the victory that His followers enjoyed when casting out demons in His name

- Deliverance cannot be understood by those who consider themselves wise or those who are prudent

- To consider yourself wise means to think that you have more knowledge and experience on an issue than others. People like this also think that their knowledge gives them the right to judge others' views

- Prudent refers to those who are overly careful and cautious; who try to act sensible or discreet. Jesus did not call us to be prudent; he called us to walk boldly in faith, to trust Him; not to rely on our own understanding but to follow and be taught by the Holy Spirit. Unfortunately most church leaders and church goers act

90

very prudently and it's not going to benefit them one bit when they have to give an account to the Lord

- God chose to reveal His authority and share His power with those who know that they are His children and totally dependent on Him

Jesus teaches that forgiveness is key to deliverance

Luke 11:4, "And forgive us our sins, For we also forgive everyone who is indebted to us. And do not lead us into temptation, But deliver us from the evil one.""

What can we learn from this scripture?

- Jesus said that we should ask for forgiveness of sins from the Father, but that we also should forgive others

- For us to receive forgiveness of sins from the Father we have to forgive those who have sinned or transgressed against us. If we are unable to forgive them, God will not forgive us. Without forgiveness of sins deliverance is not possible because there remains a debt to be settled. If you forgive others their sins, Jesus will forgive you your sins and He has already settled your debt for you

- Jesus says we should ask God not to lead us into temptation. This indicates that we have an influence over the number of trials and temptations we endure. We may choose to believe what Jesus said here is true; pray this on a daily basis and reap the benefits or we may choose to suffer temptation.

  Jesus gave us a key in this prayer to enjoy a life where He has already dealt with temptations and trials. He overcame all temptation and then told us that we should ask God on a daily basis not to be led into temptation.

  There is one major challenge that we must overcome – we get so tangled up in our own lives that our problems become insurmountable, blocking us from seeing the

Lord's hand in the situation. Then we tend to look at our own abilities and inabilities to overcome these problems rather than focusing on Christ's abilities. When we do this we fear trials and temptations because we know that we often fail and get hurt in the process.

Temptation is something that is not often talked about in churches. To be tempted means to be tested. The fact that we have to ask God not to be tested clearly shows that God tests us. I don't know about you, but I hate tests. To be tested by God means that some area in your life, where you have not been doing very well, is going to be examined. A trial will be organized for you in order for the heavenly hosts to make an analysis of your growth in the area of your weakness.

In 1 Peter 4:12-13 it says, "Beloved, do not think it strange concerning the fiery trial which is to try you, as though some strange thing happened to you; but rejoice to the extent that you partake of Christ's sufferings, that when His glory is revealed, you may also be glad with exceeding joy."

We don't just fear trials and temptations, but when they come we often view them as an attack by the enemy. The fact is that God often allows trails and temptations to cross our paths. Failure during tests and trials makes us realize that we are imperfect and in need of a Savior; and it's during these times that most people cry out to God from their hearts for help and intervention. It is dying to the idea that you can succeed on your own; or in short, it is dying to self that makes us appreciate and embrace Jesus' victory as our own!

- Jesus says we must ask to be delivered from the evil one. To deliver means to set us free from the evil one or to take us away from the evil one

Jesus casts out a spirit of infirmity

Luke 13:10-14, "Now He was teaching in one of the synagogues on the Sabbath. And behold, there was a woman who had a spirit of infirmity eighteen years, and was bent over and could in no way raise herself up. But when Jesus saw her, He called her to Him and said to her, "Woman, you are loosed from your infirmity." And He laid His hands on her, and immediately she was made straight, and glorified God. But the ruler of the synagogue answered with indignation, because Jesus had healed on the Sabbath; and he said to the crowd, "There are six days on which men ought to work; therefore come and be healed on them, and not on the Sabbath day."

What can we learn from this example?

- Jesus healed a woman on the Sabbath. The church leaders of His day didn't see the miracle but rather chose to concentrate on their own interpretation of the Biblical laws. Jesus called the church leadership hypocrites and white-washed graves because they were forcing the people to live by the laws that they, themselves, were not keeping. Church leaders today still choose to impose their own rules and regulations in their churches rather than allow the Spirit of God to minister to His people

- The spirit of infirmity had been living inside the woman for 18 years. If a spirit is not addressed and cast out, it will stay inside until the person dies, and then it will try and enter into the children or other family members. Demons also tend to attract each other. Once one has gained entrance, it opens the door for more to enter – all of them bringing their own particular manifestations and causing different problems in one's life

- The spirit of infirmity can be identified as any illness or sickness that causes weakness, frailty or a lack of power and energy. This woman had been unable to stand up straight for 18 years. Today, we'd probably see a diagnosis of severe back problems or osteoporosis

- Jesus told her that she was loosed from her infirmity and laid His hands on her. The laying on of hands to pray for healing is scriptural and the casting out of demons is done by the spoken word – instruction

- She was immediately healed and stood up straight – the very thing that she had been unable to do for 18 years, she was immediately able to do!

- She glorified God. When you have been delivered from a spirit and healed from an affliction, there is a major change in your life. You know that God has healed and delivered you and thankfulness and awe of God flood your body, mind, soul and spirit. This immediately brings you into a powerful and intimate relationship with God. It's normal for this to bubble over into praises, glorifying God

Obedience to God effects deliverance and healing

Luke 17:13-19: "And they lifted up their voices and said, "Jesus, Master, have mercy on us!" So when He saw them, He said to them, "Go, show yourselves to the priests." And so it was that as they went, they were cleansed. And one of them, when he saw that he was healed, returned, and with a loud voice glorified God, and fell down on his face at His feet, giving Him thanks. And he was a Samaritan. So Jesus answered and said, "Were there not ten cleansed? But where are the nine? Were there not any found who returned to give glory to God except this foreigner?" And He said to him, "Arise, go your way. Your faith has made you well."

What can we learn from this example?

- These men, suffering leprosy, asked the Lord for mercy and when He gave the command, they acted in faith. They took the steps in faith even though their healing only manifested on the way to the priest. Faith and obedience to God brings deliverance, cleansing and healing

- "Foreigners" to our faith, like the Samaritan, will also be delivered if they call on the Lord and show faith in Him

- The foreigner was the only one who returned and thanked Him. Jesus was not this man's Lord, but he had received something he knew he didn't deserve. God loves a thankful and appreciative heart; let us always remember never to take Jesus and His work for granted!

- This foreigner glorified Jesus with a loud voice. A miracle happened to him and at the same time he got to know the only living God! What an awesome experience this must have been for this man. He had not been brought up in this belief system and had no knowledge of religious rules and regulations to analyze and find fault with what had happened. Instead he acted the way a child would have, who had received an awesome present. This man had no inhibitions about what had happened and simply raised his voice in worship and fell down flat to glorify God for the miracle that had just happened to him

God avenges those who are persecuted

Luke 18:2-8: "...There was in a certain city a judge who did not fear God nor regard man. Now there was a widow in that city; and she came to him, saying, 'Get justice for me from my adversary.' And he would not for a while; but afterward he said within himself, 'Though I do not fear God nor regard man, yet because this widow troubles me I will avenge her, lest by her continual coming she weary me.' "Then the Lord said, "Hear what the unjust judge said. And shall God not avenge His own elect who cry out day and night to Him, though He bears long with them? I tell you that He will avenge them speedily."

What can we learn from this example?
- This story is a parable about principles. In this story we hear from a woman who continuously cried out to a worldly judge to get justice from her adversary – and in the end gets what she diligently sought

- The judge wasn't a man of God who was moved by compassion to show mercy towards the woman. He eventually gave the woman what she had been asking for, out of fear that she would continue nagging and that it would drive him crazy

- The focus of the story is that we should not give up easily but doggedly pursue what's right. The worldly judge was being worn down by a widow who cried out for justice without giving up; probably irritating the daylights out of him. However, she succeeded in what she set out to do. It's this tenacity that we should develop and apply in our lives. Today's society has grown far too accustomed to instant gratification, and not developing fruits of longsuffering and persistence

- Satan is called our adversary. In this parable Jesus encourages us not to allow Satan to go unchallenged in the injustices he brings across our paths, but rather to continuously request God to bring him to justice

- God loves us. It's His pleasure to deliver us and see a just outcome to our trials and problems. The question is: Do we have the tenacity to cry out for justice day and night?

Jesus came to save sinners

Luke 19:9-10, "And Jesus said to him, "Today salvation has come to this house, because he also is a son of Abraham; for the Son of Man has come to seek and to save that which was lost.""

What can we learn from this example?

- In this example Jesus entered Jericho and told a rich tax collector, Zacchaeus, that He would be staying at his house for the night. Everyone complained that Jesus chose a "sinners" house at which to spend the night

- Jesus came to seek and save sinners. He did not come to confirm those who think they are better than others or live holier lives than others. Your heart's attitude is seen by God and the deliverance you receive is dependent on a heart's attitude of willingness to confess sin and repent.

In the book of Luke we see how a Pharisee's heart's attitude displeases God while the sinner's heart's attitude leads to exaltation by God.

Luke 18:11-14, "The Pharisee stood and prayed thus with himself, 'God, I thank You that I am not like other men-- extortionists, unjust, adulterers, or even as this tax collector. I fast twice a week; I give tithes of all that I possess.' And the tax collector, standing afar off, would not so much as raise his eyes to heaven, but beat his breast, saying, 'God, be merciful to me a sinner!' I tell you, this man went down to his house justified rather than the other; for everyone who exalts himself will be humbled, and he who humbles himself will be exalted.'"

Jesus accuses the church leaders of being unclean within

Matthew 23:27-28: "Woe to you, scribes and Pharisees, hypocrites! For you are like whitewashed tombs which indeed appear beautiful outwardly, but inside are full of dead men's bones and all uncleanness. Even so you also outwardly appear righteous to men, but inside you are full of hypocrisy and lawlessness."

What can we learn from this example?

- Don't look at the outward beauty of others, especially those in leadership positions in the church. Keep your eyes on Jesus as your only perfect example. Many people turn away from God because of what other so-called Christians do. God is not going to excuse you in the Day of Judgment because you followed others who were supposed to lead you to Christ. He gave all of us a perfect example, Jesus! Besides, when we judge others, we will be judged by God in the same manner. Judgment belongs to God – stay clear of it!

- God sees what's inside and is not deceived by the outward appearances. Make sure that your motivation and heart's intent will be acceptable to God; if not, your works for God will not stand in the Day of Judgment

- A person may have all the knowledge of the Bible, but if they're not filled with the Holy Spirit, they're dead. If you are not filled with the Holy Spirit, you will be turned away at Heaven's Gate and will not be allowed to enter in

Jesus cast demons out of a blind and mute man

Matthew 12:22-29 says, "Then one was brought to Him who was demon-possessed, blind and mute; and He healed him, so that the blind and mute man both spoke and saw. And all the multitudes were amazed and said, "Could this be the Son of David?" Now when the Pharisees heard it they said, "This fellow does not cast out demons except by Beelzebub, the ruler of the demons."

But Jesus knew their thoughts, and said to them: "Every kingdom divided against itself is brought to desolation, and every city or house divided against itself will not stand. If Satan casts out Satan, he is divided against himself. How then will his kingdom stand? And if I cast out demons by Beelzebub, by whom do your sons cast them out? Therefore they shall be your judges. But if I cast out demons by the Spirit of God, surely the kingdom of God has come upon you. Or how can one enter a strong man's house and plunder his goods, unless he first binds the strong man? And then he will plunder his house.""

What can we learn from this example?
- Blindness and muteness is caused by demons and can be cast out of a person

- People, just like the Pharisees, who are not filled with the Holy Spirit, do not understand deliverance and will criticize and judge those who cast out demons

- Such people lack knowledge and insight and will call deliverance the work of Satan or the work done by Satan and his demons

- Demons cannot be cast out by Satan or his demons, only by the Holy Spirit and His work through those in whom He dwells

- When you minister deliverance you first have to bind the strongman before you cast out the lesser demons and reclaim lost ground

In our book, "Who are You?" we provide you with comprehensive knowledge on the principalities and powers, how to cast them out and walk the road to victory over these demons.

Jesus helps John overcome his doubts

Luke 7:19-23, "And John, calling two of his disciples to him, sent them to Jesus, saying, "Are You the Coming One, or do we look for another?" When the men had come to Him, they said, "John the Baptist has sent us to You, saying, 'Are You the Coming One, or do we look for another?' "

And that very hour He cured many of infirmities, afflictions, and evil spirits; and to many blind He gave sight. Jesus answered and said to them, "Go and tell John the things you have seen and heard: that the blind see, the lame walk, the lepers are cleansed, the deaf hear, the dead are raised, the poor have the gospel preached to them. And blessed is he who is not offended because of Me.""

What can we learn from this example?

- God revealed to John who Jesus was. In John 1:33-34 we read of John acknowledging Jesus as the Son of God, "I did not know Him, but He who sent me to baptize with water said to me, 'Upon whom you see the Spirit descending, and remaining on Him, this is He who baptizes with the Holy Spirit.' And I have seen and testified that this is the Son of God." This scripture makes it clear that John knew who Jesus was, yet at a time when he was in prison, being severely tested, he doubted. Those who receive Godly revelation must expect to be tested. Satan and his demons will try and rob you of Godly revelation

- The signs and miracles that Jesus displayed also testified of who He was

- Some of the miracles, signs and wonders performed by Jesus and His followers, might not conform to what we think they should. For example, Jesus healed on the Sabbath; this did not fit in with the Pharisees' interpretation of Biblical laws. Jesus had no qualms calling the Pharisees white washed graves, yet many people today frown on any Godly words spoken against church leadership – it offends them. Jesus' response to this attitude is that those who are not offended by Him (and His followers who are called to do the same things Jesus did) will be blessed

- Jesus cured people when He cast evil spirits out of them

Guideline on how to cast demons out

It is important to be led by the Holy Spirit when you cast out demons. Each deliverance is unique and will be different. There are, however, some general guidelines that will help you to ensure that you don't forget to address important issues. The guidelines provided below pertain to a religious spirit and cannot be followed to the letter for deliverance of all spirits. If you want to obtain more detailed guidelines for the different principalities and powers you will come across in deliverances, please read our book entitled "Who are You". It contains a practical deliverance guideline for all the principalities and powers mentioned in the Bible.

Identification of the spirit
- Identify the work of the spirit in your life

Forgiveness

- Make a list of the names of those people you need to forgive, including yourself, your parents and ancestors. Forgive those who have sinned against you and release them. Ask God to forgive you, as you have forgiven those who sinned against you

- Ask God to forgive you for being a stumbling block to others and that you allowed this spirit to operate through you

Repentance of sins

- Repent for harboring the spirit. An example of a prayer of repentance:
  - Lord I ask You, in the Name of Jesus Christ, to forgive my ancestors and I for allowing this spirit to operate through us
- Repent and turn away from the sins caused by this spirit, which are:
  - Spirit of idolatry
  - Loveless spirit
  - Spirit of death
  - Spirit of division
  - Spirit of legalism
  - Spirit of condemnation
  - Spirit of confusion
  - Anti-Christ spirit
  - Spirit of unbelief
  - Spirit of control (Jezebel)
  - Spirit of submission (Ahab)
  - Judgmental spirit
  - Spirit of self-righteousness
  - Spirit of pride
  - Spirit of criticism
  - Spirit of perfectionism

- Spirit of rejection
- Spirit of self-rejection
- Spirit of fear of rejection
- Spirit of error
- Spirit of doubt
- Spirit of discord
- Spirit of fear
- Spirit of anxiety
- Spirit of stress
- Spirit of rejection
- Spirit of self-rejection
- Rebellion
- Manipulation
- Spirit of deception
- Spirit of striving
- Spirit of greed
- Spirit of uncleanness

Sever ungodly soul-ties and ungodly spiritual contracts

- Identify all soul-ties that have occurred due to ungodly sexual relationships. Cut each of these soul-ties individually and declare them null and void. Declare that the demons that used these soul-ties to transfer from person to person will have no more rights to do this. Seal these soul-ties with the anointing of the Holy Spirit and / or the blood of Jesus
- Make the following declaration:
  - In the Name of Jesus Christ, I declare a divorce with this spirit
  - I tear up any contracts and revoke any rights my ancestors or I gave these spirits in our life and declare them nullified
  - I declare that I take all rights back in the name of Jesus Christ who came in the flesh

Deal with curses, rituals and altars

- Ask the Lord to lift any curses that He has allowed to come upon you because of these sins. For example: Father, in Jesus Name I ask that You will remove the following curses and fruits in my life as a result of my ancestors' and my own involvement with this spirit:
    - Curse of death
    - Curse that the plunderers will despoil you
    - Curse that you will be given into the hands of your enemies
    - Curse of calamity
    - Curse of great distress on you
    - Curse of oppression
    - Curse of harassment
    - Curse that you will live in the midst of your enemies and God will not deliver your enemies into your hand. (Judges 2:23)
    - Curse of destruction Exodus 22:20
    - Curse of loss of property
    - Curse of double mindedness
    - Curse of spiritual blindness
    - Curse of spiritual death
    - Curse of being tormented with all the plagues of Egypt
    - Curse of insanity
    - Curse of infirmity
    - Curse of the utmost judgment
    - Curse of slavery
    - Curse of demonic affliction and torment

  I pray that You will change each one of these curses into blessings in the life of my family

- Ask God to forgive your ancestors and yourself for partaking in evil rituals and for offering the blood of the innocent to idols

- Cancel all rituals that have been performed against you and your family in the name of Jesus. Seek God's face and ask Him if there are any specific counter / prophetic actions He wants you to perform regarding these rituals
- Pronounce destruction over the altars of this spirit in your life, declare that you are a temple of the living God and that He alone reigns as King in your life
- Ask the Lord to remove all leaven that caused you to walk under the control of this spirit, from your habits of thinking, your will, emotions and your body

Bind and cast the demons out

- Bind the principality. Then bind the power. Suggested wording: "I bind you (name of power) _____ in the name of Jesus Christ who came in the flesh." If you have identified these sins as bloodline sins, address it as follows: "I bind you (name of power) _____ in the name of Jesus Christ who came in the flesh in the fourth, third, second and in this generation. I speak death over your roots, branches and fruits in the life of _____ (name of the person being delivered)"
- Command the demon to leave and continue to do so until it leaves. This is where you have to operate in Godly discernment. Ask the Lord to help you discern when the demon has left. From experience, we have learned that the following will help you in your warfare:
  - Remind the demon that you are standing in the authority of Jesus Christ and that the demon is actually facing Christ and not you
  - Remind the demon of the victory that we have through the blood of Christ that flowed on the cross
  - Remind the demon that all his rights have been taken away
  - Remind the demon that the person being delivered does not want it to reside in them anymore. You may even request the person going through

deliverance to say the words out loud: (Name of power) _____, I don't want you inside of me. Leave me in the name of Jesus Christ who came in the flesh

- Quote scripture, as the Spirit of the Lord leads you. Examples of scriptures to quote:
- Deuteronomy 32:30 "one chases a thousand, And two put ten thousand to flight"
- Matthew 16:19 "And I will give you the keys of the kingdom of heaven, and whatever you bind on earth will be bound in heaven, and whatever you loose on earth will be loosed in heaven."
- Revelation 12:11 "And they overcame him by the blood of the Lamb and by the word of their testimony, and they did not love their lives to the death."
- Matthew 28:18 "All authority has been given to Me in heaven and on earth."
- Luke 10:19 "Behold, I give you the authority to trample on serpents and scorpions, and over all the power of the enemy, and nothing shall by any means hurt you."
- Sing worship songs or praise the Lord
- Pray with understanding and pray in tongues

- Perform any prophetic actions that God gives you, for example:
  - Thrusting with the Sword of the Spirit
  - Walking around the person
  - Placing your hand on the person, as the Lord leads you. Always keeping in mind the dignity of the person and what is proper and acceptable
  - Removing yokes and false mantles or bondages, as the Lord leads you
- When the demon has left, thank the Lord and ask Him to command his angels to remove the demon and to take it to where the Lord requires it next

- Bind and cast out only those demons in the following list that you identify as having assisted this demonic power in its work within the person being ministered to: (Following the same steps as used to cast out the power) Spirit of death, spirit of infirmity, spirit of division, anti-Christ spirit, spirit of control (Jezebel), judgmental spirit, spirit of self-righteousness, spirit of pride, spirit of criticism, spirit of legalism, spirit of perfectionism, spirit of error, spirit of unbelief, spirit of greed, spirit of uncleanness, spirit of doubt, spirit of confusion, spirit of discord, spirit of condemnation, spirit of fear, spirit of anxiety, spirit of stress, spirit of rejection, spirit of self-rejection
- Bind and cast out each individual spirit in the name of Jesus Christ who came in the flesh
- Lastly, bind and cast out the following principalities: Apollyon, Beast, Beelzebub

Restoration and healing

- Invite the Lord Jesus Christ to take His rightful place on the throne of your heart
- This is a good time to pray for the infilling of the Holy Spirit. Ask the Lord to fill you with the Spirit of adoption into the Body of Christ
- This is also the right time to pray for any physical and emotional healing that is required. We use olive oil as a symbol of the Holy Spirit and we lay our hands on the sick and pray for healing in the name of Jesus Christ, who came in the flesh
- Identify the fruits of the Spirit that counteract the sins you were involved in and set your mind on growing in these areas
- Ask the Lord to help you renew your mind and to bring you to a place of obedience where you will find scriptures and apply them when you find yourself under spiritual attack. Renew your mind by consciously deciding against sinning. Gather scriptures that counteract the particular

sins that plagued you and quote them in times of temptation until the urge to fall into sin flees from you

- Revoke and take back all rights Satan has to control your life, will, mind, emotions and body and submit them to the Lord
- Counteract the fruits of the spirit of lust by praying and spending time in God's presence, and by exercising self-control
- Find out who you are in Christ by identifying verses in the Bible. Memorize some of these verses and quote them when you find yourself under spiritual attack
- Quit looking at your own inabilities and failures and walk in God's abilities and righteousness
- Expect spiritual opposition and that the spirits that left will try to return – be alert and aware. Satan will try and attack you with self-centeredness and compromise. Counteract these attacks by consciously dying to your own will and submitting to what God wants in every area of your life
- Do not waste time under condemnation
- Pick up the sword of the Spirit and war against the powers, principalities and their fruits in your life!

Equipping and Aftercare

- Share with the person the keys to retain their deliverance, as shared in the book "Who are You". In fact, it would be excellent for this person to have a copy of this book and to read it cover to cover. This will ensure that they obtain much needed knowledge and will not perish due to a lack of thereof. (Hosea 4:6)

- Please keep in mind, and share with the person, that they will be tired after deliverance. They might also continue experiencing minor manifestations for the next couple of days. This is normal and they need to press into the presence of the Lord and rest in Him during this time. This is why it is called warfare – a spiritual battle has

107

taken place and all those involved will feel the effects on their physical bodies

Scriptures to use against this spirit

- Matthew 11:28-30 "Come to Me, all you who labor and are heavy laden, and I will give you rest. Take My yoke upon you and learn from Me, for I am gentle and lowly in heart, and you will find rest for your souls. For My yoke is easy and My burden is light."

CHAPTER FIVE

They will speak with new tongues

Why speak in tongues

To speak in tongues builds your faith. Jude 1:20, "But you, beloved, building yourselves up on your most holy faith, praying in the Holy Spirit". To speak in a tongue for the first time is a tremendous boost to your faith and probably one of the most awesome experiences you'll ever have. It is when the unfamiliar sounds roll off your tongue for the first time that you will be filled with wonder. You will know that this has never happened to you before and that it is not something that you can make happen by sheer willpower. You will know that it is from, and worked through, the Spirit of God. It is an intensely personal experience and will bring the certainty that God knows you; not just by name, but knows you inside out. You will realize that there is nothing that you can hide from God; that He has access to your deepest secrets and desires. You will also realize that despite this, God has chosen you as vessel to work through.

How wonderful it must have been for the disciples when they first spoke in tongues, as recorded in Acts 2:4, "And they were all filled with the Holy Spirit and began to speak with other tongues, as the Spirit gave them utterance." Just imagine the group of disciples crying out to God in anguish, in one accord. "Lord, help us...you were our Leader and now you are gone. What should we do? Lord, you taught us so much, it's burnt into our hearts and we cannot just let it go...what should we do? Please Lord, you told us to come here and wait....Come Lord Jesus – help us!"

All of a sudden a sound fills the air. The sound of a mighty wind echoed the tempestuous cries in their hearts. It seemed as if the powerful wind vibrated through the room causing the foundations of the building to shake. The men, some lying face down on the floor, others kneeling with their heads bowed to the ground hardly noticed. As if in one accord, the tone of their voices changed. Their desperate pleading was replaced by shouts of heartfelt elation. Their spirit-man acknowledged the arrival of God's presence in the room. They stood up, their faces turned to heaven, shining with an inner radiance. Upon their heads could be seen, what appeared to be flames which flared in intensity, as their shouts of joy rose above the sound of the wind. Their eyes intently fixed upon something or someone, invisible to others. Tears of sorrow turned to tears of joy. They were communing with God through the Holy Spirit for the first time in their lives. The sounds of heavenly language filled the air, as all men and angels present in the upper room worshipped the one and only God, in Spirit and in truth. The Holy Spirit had arrived; the Promise had been poured out for the first time!

The heavens were opened above the upper room on that day to such an extent that no person in the area could resist the draw of the Spirit. From all around, the sound of the wind, mingled with the voices of pure worship and praise, drew the attention. The people felt themselves inexplicably drawn to this sound. As the multitudes in the crowd pushed forward, to find out for themselves what was happening, curiosity gave way to wonder. ""Look, are not all these who speak Galileans? And how is it that we hear, each in our own language in which we were born?" they asked each other in astonishment. "We hear them speaking in our own tongues the wonderful works of God. Whatever could this mean?" they wanted to know; whilst others mockingly said, "They are full of new wine."

Hardly had the Holy Spirit been poured out for the first time, when Satan launched his first attack. True to his nature, the "Accuser of the brethren" planted the seed in man's mind, that those who speak in tongues must be doing something wrong – perhaps drunk with new wine! Have you heard or even partaken in attacking the work of the Holy Spirit, by speaking out against the signs that Jesus said we should have? This is a good time to repent before God and ask Him forgiveness for this sin. You cannot speak out against the signs, and then, at a later stage expect to receive them when you come to the realization that you need them. I have often found that people have thought negatively, spoken out against, or openly accused those who display the signs of the Holy Spirit, as operating within Satan's domain. These people usually find it difficult to start flowing in signs.

You can only speak in a Godly tongue when you are filled with the Holy Spirit. To speak in tongues, means that you are speaking in a spiritual language and the words spoken will not make any sense unless the Holy Spirit gives you the interpretation. To speak in tongues is to commune with God. You do not speak words according to your own mind but according to the Spirit. The Holy Spirit prays through you when you speak in tongues. In Romans 8:26-27 it says, "Likewise the Spirit also helps in our weaknesses. For we do not know what we should pray for as we ought, but the Spirit Himself makes intercession for us with groanings which cannot be uttered. Now He who searches the hearts knows what the mind of the Spirit is, because He makes intercession for the saints according to the will of God." Isn't it wonderful to know that God Himself perfects our prayers by praying through us by His Holy Spirit? These prayers are always heard by God and acted upon, because they are according to the direct will of God. The more you pray in tongues, the more you have the Spirit of God interceding on your behalf before our Father.

When we pray in tongues, we are investing time in our spirit-man. We are body, soul and spirit. If we neglect to feed our bodies, it will eventually die, the same happens with our spirit-man. We need to feed it and allow it to drink from the river of living water which flows from God's throne. This means we need to pray in the spirit. This edifies your spirit-man; it fills you with light and life; it keeps you in a spirit-sensitive state where you discern between right and wrong, and even to discern different spirits in the spiritual world. Praying in tongues brings you into the presence of God and allows the glory of God to flow through you. There are so many benefits to praying in tongues – I want to urge you, if you do not pray in tongues, seek God's face and ask the Lord to give you a burning desire for more of Him. This sign is free of charge and will benefit you greatly!

Praying in tongues brings you to a place where your focus is on God and not on any worldly thing. It is so easy for us to get caught up in our circumstances and the issues that influence our lives. It is at times like this that we usually feel overwhelmed and out of control. The truth is that we usually are out of control when we look at our circumstances. Just as Peter started sinking when he looked at the waves instead of at Jesus, we too start sinking when we focus on the circumstances instead of on the Lord's abilities. Praying in tongues helps us to focus on God's abilities instead of our inabilities. Let's face it, we could lose all the things that we surround ourselves with in a second, if it was not for God's favor, mercy and grace. Everything we are surrounded with, even the breath, we breathe, is subject to God's will. Nothing is a certainty except God and His love for us. Are you at a place where you know and trust God's love for you? If not, you need to spend more time praying in tongues.

I remember a time in my life when I was extremely lonely and the cares of raising a child on my own felt more than I could handle. I joined a prayer group at the time and enjoyed the presence of the Lord as we all spent hours in praise and worship before the Lord. After spending such wonderful time with the Lord, I often remember feeling as if someone had taken a tooth brush and brushed me clean inside and out. Praying in tongues does not only build us up, but we also receive new strength and energy to face the world.

I also often find while I pray in tongues that the Lord shares new perspectives and creative ways of dealing with issues in my life. In the past I used to spend hours mulling my problems over in my mind, trying to decide on the best way to resolve them. I have however found that God is much better at handling my problems than I am. He has a much clearer view of the issues and knows exactly what I should do. When I pray in tongues and wait on God, these revelations are released to me and I often stand in awe of how small these problems shrink in the presence of God.

Spending time praying in tongues is spending time with God. God created us to have a deep love relationship with Him. You cannot have a meaningful relationship if there is no communication. Praying in tongues is praying from the deepest areas of your heart and soul. It gives meaning to the words "deep calls unto deep" in Psalm 42:7. It is intimate communication where the words in our normal language fall far too short to describe adequately. It is a communication in emotion more than it is a communication of words. The words uttered will have no carnal meaning yet your soul man will be filled with deep emotion.

Praying in tongues is a powerful weapon in spiritual warfare as is seen in Ephesians 6:17-18, "...and the sword of the Spirit, which is the word of God; praying always with all prayer and supplication in the Spirit, being watchful to this end with all perseverance and supplication for all the saints...". Hebrew 4:12 also calls the word of God living and powerful, "For the word of God is living and powerful, and sharper than any two-edged sword, piercing even to the division of soul and spirit, and of joints and marrow, and is a discerner of the thoughts and intents of the heart." For people involved in spiritual warfare there should not be any doubts or questions concerning the signs and gifts of God. Many Christians doubt whether the signs Jesus spoke of, are Godly; but once you enter the spiritual battlefield, there is no place for these doubts. Such doubts will open you up to attack by Satan.

Demons fear God's voice; they recognize the authority, the anointing and the power in God's voice. They greatly fear when they hear God's children praying in tongues, because they realize that the words spoken are done so by the Spirit of God. These powerful words, together with quoting Scriptures constitute the sword of the Spirit that we wield against the enemy. When you pray in tongues, as led by the Spirit of God while doing deliverance, the Spirit of the Lord is actually interceding for the person you are ministering to. These prayers are perfect prayers and will not return to God void, but will accomplish all that they have been sent out to do as is described in Isaiah 55:11, "So shall My word be that goes forth from My mouth; It shall not return to Me void, But it shall accomplish what I please, And it shall prosper in the thing for which I sent it."

God knows the power of the spoken word, which is something we as His children need to learn. God created the universe by speaking it into being. We have been created in God's image and filled with His Spirit, who prays through us. Are you now starting to realize the creative power there is in the words you allow the Spirit of God to speak through you? Are you starting to understand why it is important to speak in tongues day and night without ceasing? Do you realize why it grieves the Spirit of the Lord when we, as His children, speak out against the work of His Spirit? If you have ever criticized or spoken out against the signs Jesus said we should display, I urge you to take some time now to ask the Lord for forgiveness and to request Him to grant you to flow in these signs.

According to Romans 8:26, praying in tongues helps us to deal with our infirmities in an effective manner. The word "infirmity" used in Romans 8:26 is the same word that is used when Jesus bore our infirmities and sicknesses in Matthew 8:17. The word "infirmity" refers to:

- our lack of strength or vitality

- a weakness or character flaw

- any medical condition that causes a lack of strength or vitality

What is so encouraging about these scriptures is that when we are confronted with infirmities we usually feel too weak and often lack the knowledge to deal with it effectively. If you pray in your tongue, you are allowing the Spirit of God to deal with the issue in a manner that is 100% effective and guaranteed to work. Are you sick or do you have to minister to someone who is sick – pray in tongues, the Bible says it will work!

One thing about praying in tongues which is important to remember is that you are praying in the Spirit and not with your mind. It is true that we do not always know how to pray or what to pray for, but the Spirit of God knows and helps us pray correctly and effectively. This is especially true when we are too close to a difficult situation and don't know what to pray for, or when we have to pray for people we don't know well. The Bible says that the Spirit intercedes with groaning which cannot be uttered. I am a woman and of nature I am emotional. I've heard woman groan in childbirth and people groan in dire pain, and every time I hear these groanings, it has a profound effect on me. I find it very comforting that I have a Friend in the Holy Spirit who can intercede on my behalf in such a powerful manner.

A lot of people reason that speaking in tongues is simply speaking another language that already exists on earth. In 1 Corinthians 14:2 it says, "For he who speaks in a tongue does not speak to men but to God, for no one understands him; however, in the spirit he speaks mysteries." I do believe that when you speak in tongues it is done through the Holy Spirit and that the Holy Spirit gives interpretation and understanding of what was spoken to whomever He will. This also explains why the crowds in Acts 2 understood the tongues – because the Holy Spirit granted them interpretation. Interpretation is usually granted to a few people at a time, who will all testify to the same spoken words. It has often happened to me that I would be given an interpretation of a tongue, but before I could share it, someone else would give the exact interpretation and I would merely confirm that it was correct and true.

Isn't it amazing that Jesus told us in Mark 16:17 that we, as His followers, will be speaking in new tongues, yet there is such a large group of those claiming to follow Him who contradict His own words. A lot of these people use the words of Paul in 1 Corinthians 14:22-33 to refute Jesus' own words on the subject. Now I speak for myself when I say, I'll go with what Jesus Himself said, because it is to Him that I have to give account one day.

Paul's teachings in fact do not contradict Jesus but can be twisted to be misunderstood, and this is a gap used by Satan to rob those who want to follow Jesus in fullness and in truth. 1 Corinthians 14:4-5 says, "He who speaks in a tongue edifies himself, but he who prophesies edifies the church. I wish you all spoke with tongues, but even more that you prophesied; for he who prophesies is greater than he who speaks with tongues, unless indeed he interprets, that the church may receive edification." In this scripture Paul says that you are edified when you speak in tongues and that Paul wishes that all spoke in tongues.

Paul teaches on the gifts of the Spirit, of which he mentions tongues, healing, faith, words of wisdom, words of knowledge, miracles, prophecy, discerning of spirits and interpretation of tongues as different gifts of the Spirit. Paul was dealing with issues which threatened to cause disunity in the church at that time. Some people were operating in the gifts of the Holy Spirit and others were not yet at that point of maturity. This caused jealousy and pride to surface. Paul did not want the gifts of the Holy Spirit to become the focus of the church, in place of God. He tried to explain the importance of the different gifts of the Spirit to a group of people who did not know much about Christianity at that time. Paul's words should not be misinterpreted as conflicting Jesus' own words on the importance of signs; after all, Paul was a follower of Jesus while Jesus is the Ultimate Authority. In 1 Corinthians 14:18 Paul confirms his belief in the importance of speaking in tongues, "I thank my God I speak with tongues more than you all".

Paul recognized the fact that not all people flow in all gifts. This does not reflect on the unavailability of these gifts to all people. It rather highlights the different places at which we find ourselves on the path of holiness. Jesus clearly stated that we will display all the signs, if we believe in Him and follow Him. When you look at those who follow Jesus at a specific point in time, you will find some who do not yet speak in tongues. It does not mean that they will never speak in tongues; in fact the tongues are there for the speaking. They have to receive it just as you would receive a gift, before it becomes yours. Likewise Paul talks about faith as a gift. We should all have faith, yet we do not all display the same level of faith all the time. This is where the Holy Spirit gives as it pleases God.

In 1 Corinthians 14:22 Paul says, "Therefore tongues are for a sign, not to those who believe but to unbelievers". There are a few reasons why Paul would have made this statement. Firstly, people who already speak in tongues know that it's real and powerful. They are already convinced and have therefore become believers of the value of speaking in tongues. When believers speak in tongues, it identifies them as followers of Jesus, especially to any unbelievers present. Secondly, it highlights the necessity to pray in tongues; not just amongst Spirit-filled Christians, but also in meetings where unbelievers are present. We are given signs not just for our own edification but to draw those who do not know God towards Him.

In 1 Corinthians 14:14-15 Paul says, "For if I pray in a tongue, my spirit prays, but my understanding is unfruitful. What is the conclusion then? I will pray with the spirit, and I will also pray with the understanding. I will sing with the spirit, and I will also sing with the understanding." In these scriptures Paul comes to a conclusion and shares it with those he taught. His conclusion shows that praying in tongues is important because you don't pray according to your earthly desires or understanding. He further explains that it is good to pray with understanding where groups of people meet in order for all to agree on what has been prayed. He stipulates that praying in tongues should not be forbidden in group meetings but that such praying should be followed by interpretation in order for all to agree on what was being said.

Neuroscientists have done numerous studies on speaking in tongues and I'd like to share a few of their findings that I found interesting.

- When speaking in tongues, the activity in the area of control in your brain decreases. I believe this happens because you submit your mind and control to God when you allow the Holy Spirit to pray through you

- Activity in the language center of the brain decreases. I believe this happens because it is not a language consisting of words with meaning, but it is a communing with God consisting of emotion. This also explains the next point

- Activity in the emotional center of the brain increases.

- When speaking in tongues, you are not in a state of hypnosis, in a trance, in a state of lower mental capacity or mentally ill

The above information was obtained from the following website: http://en.wikipedia.org/wiki/Glossolalia

How to speak in new tongues

Here are some guidelines for speaking in tongues:

- You must be filled with the Holy Spirit

- You must desire spiritual gifts

- You must repent and ask forgiveness for speaking out against spiritual gifts if you have done so

- Ask anointed children of God to pray with you. Allow them to lay hands on you to receive your new tongue

- It helps your spirit man to receive new tongues when you are in an atmosphere of worship to God. Before praying for your tongue, meditate on the goodness and might of God. Play worship music and allow your spirit man to draw close to God

- Ask God for the gift of speaking in tongues

- Allow your heart to be focused on God

- Move into His presence and allow your heart to worship Him. You can start out your worship in your native language but when you run out of words to say, speak the sounds that flow from your spirit man. It is from the feeling or flow of worship and communication of your spirit-man with God that your tongue will come into obedience to commune in Spirit and not with words formed in your mind. If you find it difficult to find sounds to say at first, it is ok to say a few sounds of what those who are speaking in tongues around you. This will help you to take that step in faith. After all, it is not about the sounds but about the commune of your spirit man with God. You can trust God, He will not give you a snake when you ask for bread – if you ask Him for a tongue, He will protect you and give it to you

- Take a step in faith and speak the sounds you hear in your head, whilst you are in God's presence. These sounds will not be words of meaning. If you do not speak these sounds, nothing will happen. We have found from experience that it is best to speak out loud and clear and continue for as long as possible. This will make it easier next time around when you speak in your tongue

- Do not evaluate or concentrate on what the sounds sound like that comes out of your mouth. That is not what is important. What is important is the spiritual communication between your spirit and God's Spirit

- Allow the sounds to flow from your lips like a river of water. Do not check or evaluate it. Rather concentrate on the flow of power that you will feel released to you from God. This will edify your spirit man

- To speak in tongues cannot be forced. The Spirit of God gives the utterance. You are therefore not in control but God is. The Spirit of God will give you utterance at the right time. From experience we know that the right time is when you allow your spirit man to reach out and commune with God. This usually happens in a relaxed atmosphere, where you feel safe and comfortable

- Do not give up – tongues are there for all of us and Jesus expects us to have this sign

CHAPTER SIX

They will take up serpents

Throughout the Bible the serpent is the symbol used to describe and represent Satan and his demons. In Genesis 3 we first come across a talking serpent that tempts Eve to disobey God. This is the first time that Satan reveals himself to mankind and he was successful in breaking up a good relationship between God and man.

In Exodus 4 we read about signs that God gave Moses, to strengthen his faith. God promises to be with him on the mission He sent him on – to free God's people. It is very interesting to note that out of all possible signs God could have given Moses, He chose to change Moses' rod into a serpent. Moses got such a fright that he fled the scene. In Exodus 4:4 God gives Moses a command that is contrary to what any man would naturally do, "Then the LORD said to Moses, "Reach out your hand and take it by the tail" (and he reached out his hand and caught it, and it became a rod in his hand)". Why a snake, you might ask? I believe that God wanted Moses to realize that the very representation of Satan on earth – the snake – was what led to man's fall in sin, but with God's help, Moses could "take up the serpent" and control it! The translation of the words "*take up*" in Mark 16:18 is the same Greek word translated "*be removed*" in Mark 11:23. The meaning is not to charm snakes, but rather to remove demons.

What is so amazing about the command to "take up the serpent" is that God used the same symbol twice through Moses. In Numbers 21:5-8 we read how discontentment led to rebellion amongst the Israelites, "And the people spoke against God and against Moses: "Why have you brought us up out of Egypt to die in the wilderness? For there is no food and no water, and our soul loathes this worthless bread." So the LORD sent fiery serpents among the people, and they bit the people; and many of the people of Israel died. Therefore the people came to Moses, and said, "We have sinned, for we have spoken against the LORD and against you; pray to the LORD that He take away the serpents from us." So Moses prayed for the people. Then the LORD said to Moses, "Make a fiery serpent, and set it on a pole; and it shall be that everyone who is bitten, when he looks at it, shall live." Why would God give such a strange solution to

126

their problem? God did not change their circumstances at this stage, all that the people gained by looking at the fiery serpent, was to live and not die.

I believe that the serpent on the pole reminded the people of the sin they committed. The symbol of their sin was lifted up above them and it had the power of life and death over them. If they chose to look at the fiery serpent, or the sin that they committed, they received life and if they chose not to look at the sin that caused this misery in their lives, they died. This explanation is in line with what Jesus says in Mark 16:17: "…they will take up serpents". We, as Jesus' followers, are called on to constantly confront sin in our own lives (look at the fiery serpent) and those who walk a path of holiness with us. We are not supposed to tolerate sin and allow it to fester and multiply in our lives. When sin is exposed, or we become aware of it in our lives, we have to take it up and deal with it. If we choose to "look at the sin", we will live but if we choose not to "look at the sin" we will die.

In the book of Psalm, David also talks about the deliverance we will enjoy through God. In Psalm 91:13 we see that that serpent has been placed under our feet through the involvement of God, "You shall tread upon the lion and the cobra, The young lion and the serpent you shall trample underfoot."

In John 3:14-15 Jesus says, "And as Moses lifted up the serpent in the wilderness, even so must the Son of Man be lifted up, that whoever believes in Him should not perish but have eternal life." Our deliverance is only possible through Jesus and the price He paid for the sins we committed against our Father. We have a choice in the matter; we may choose to daily take up the serpents in our lives, and live; or we may choose to live with the serpents and die. What will your choice be today? Will you choose to apply the forgiveness we enjoy through repentance, in Jesus and rule over sin; or remain immobile, and die?

CHAPTER SEVEN

If they drink anything deadly

We live in a world where sin has become a way of life. Illness and disease are mostly attributed to physical reasons that can be proven and treated scientifically. The fact that illness and disease have a spiritual cause and treatment is hardly ever considered. Very few Christians know or believe that sin causes illness and disease, even though the Bible contains many examples that show that what we eat or drink can harm us from a spiritual perspective. Numbers 5:27-28 shows that water that is cursed can cause a sinner to become ill, "When he has made her drink the water, then it shall be, if she has defiled herself and behaved unfaithfully toward her husband, that the water that brings a curse will enter her and become bitter, and her belly will swell, her thigh will rot, and the woman will become a curse among her people. But if the woman has not defiled herself, and is clean, then she shall be free and may conceive children."

In Exodus 15:23-26 we read about a test with which God tested the Israelites, "Now when they came to Marah, they could not drink the waters of Marah, for they were bitter. Therefore the name of it was called Marah. And the people complained against Moses, saying, "What shall we drink?" So he cried out to the LORD, and the LORD showed him a tree. When he cast it into the waters, the waters were made sweet. There He made a statute and an ordinance for them, and there He tested them, and said, "If you diligently heed the voice of the LORD your God and do what is right in His sight, give ear to His commandments and keep all His statutes, I will put none of the diseases on you which I have brought on the Egyptians. For I am the LORD who heals you.""

In this example, God tests the attitude and obedience of His children. What He found was a nation without faith and quick to complain. I wonder what God finds when He tests us these days. When I look around me, I see the same thing Moses saw at Marah many years ago – people who are without faith and quick to complain. God loves us and He wants us to escape from bondage and enjoy a restored relationship with Him. During this deliverance process, we will face tests from God. God does not test us because He needs proof that we are worthy; He tests us because we need opportunities to grow in faith to realize that He is worthy and faithful. In this test the Israelites failed miserably yet God still made a way for them. God will make a way for you in every test. The key to passing your test is to realize that there is a spiritual reason behind every test. Once you find the spiritual reason, it becomes easy to see what needs to happen to pass the physical test.

God gave Moses a very unscientific method to sweeten the water. God's ways must drive scientists crazy! There is no way that we can explain God and His ways with our minds or by facts. God is Spirit and it's only through the Holy Spirit that we get to know Him. It is of the utmost importance for us to realize that the spiritual influences the physical. No scientist will be able to explain how curses written on paper and mixed with water can cause a sinner to become sick or die, nor will they be able to explain how bitter water becomes sweet by casting a tree into it. Our God is Spirit and He entices us through tests to become more aware of the world He lives in. He loves us and desires to be in a living relationship with us. For this to happen, we need to step into His realm – the spiritual.

We need to realize that we have become totally unbalanced. All we see and do is focused on the physical. When tests come our way we look at the mountains in front of us and we want to run away. Our eyes are constantly fixed on the problem instead of the Savior. In doing so, we empower the work of Satan and his demons in our lives. We anger God, who allows us to be tested and tried by demons and through our lack of faith and disobedience cause God to curse us. It is at times like this that we enter the spiritual battlegrounds. Through God's curses, all the plagues that besieged Egypt are unleashed upon us, and due to our lack of knowledge of the spiritual realm we become sick and enslaved. In 1 Corinthians 10:20-22 we learn that, "You cannot drink the cup of the Lord and the cup of demons; you cannot partake of the Lord's table and of the table of demons. Or do we provoke the Lord to jealousy? Are we stronger than He?" Whose cup do you choose to drink from today? Do you choose God's cup filled with blessings; or do you choose the cup of demons that will cause you to become sick and die.

Jesus already drank of the cup of death in order for us to have life. We have a choice only because Jesus made a way for us. When we partake of communion we declare openly that we accept the price that Jesus paid for us. Through the death of Jesus we have received life, but if we partake of this cup in an unworthy manner we will become weak, sick and die! This is confirmed in 1 Corinthians 11:25-30, "In the same manner He also took the cup after supper, saying, "This cup is the new covenant in My blood. This do, as often as you drink it, in remembrance of Me." For as often as you eat this bread and drink this cup, you proclaim the Lord's death till He comes. Therefore whoever eats this bread or drinks this cup of the Lord in an unworthy manner will be guilty of the body and blood of the Lord. But let a man examine himself, and so let him eat of the bread and drink of the cup. For he who eats and drinks in an unworthy manner eats and drinks judgment to himself, not discerning the Lord's body. For this reason many are weak and sick among you, and many sleep."

In 2 Kings 4:38-41 we read an example where people had soup that had poison in it, "And Elisha returned to Gilgal, and there was a famine in the land. Now the sons of the prophets were sitting before him; and he said to his servant, "Put on the large pot, and boil stew for the sons of the prophets." So one went out into the field to gather herbs, and found a wild vine, and gathered from it a lapful of wild gourds, and came and sliced them into the pot of stew, though they did not know what they were. Then they served it to the men to eat. Now it happened, as they were eating the stew, that they cried out and said, "Man of God, there is death in the pot!" And they could not eat it. So he said, "Then bring some flour." And he put it into the pot, and said, "Serve it to the people, that they may eat." And there was nothing harmful in the pot." This example shows that poison will not harm you when you involve God.

I've personally experienced God's supernatural protection on several occasions when dealing with poison. Being a deliverance minister, Satan, his demons and the Satanists and witches, have tried to poison me on at least five different occasions that I know of. I'm still here because God has not allowed the poison to harm me. We are quick to pray God's blessing over our food but how often do we pray His blessing over that which we drink. Our bodies consist of approximately 70% water. A rough calculation of an average adult's water requirement equates to a 9 oz glass per waking hour. That should have you praying over your water at least once an hour. The question is – do you? I know I don't, but I do know that Satanists and witches pray every 4 hours, day and night. During their time of prayer they curse our health, our relationships and everything that the Lord has entrusted to us. They also astral travel into our homes and poison our food and drink. How protected are we against these workers of iniquity if we do not even know what they are up to? I truly believe that many of us have walked in the sign "if they drink anything deadly, it will by no means hurt them" without realizing it.

In another example, we read in 1 Kings 13:21-25 about the death of a prophet of God because he ate and drank in a place where God commanded him not to. The prophet was deceived and subsequently disobeyed the commandment of God. He did not die because the food and drink was poisonous but because he failed to obey God's commandment. It is very clear that what we eat or drink is influenced by the spiritual. If our deeds and attitude display obedience, faith and love for God, our food and drink will bless our bodies – regardless of any of our enemies' attempts to kill us through what we consume. On the other hand, if we disobey God and display a lack of faith or love for Him, curses on perfectly good food will cause us to become weak, sick or even die.

CHAPTER EIGHT

They will lay hands on the sick

Introduction

Jesus also came to heal the sick. In the Bible we read of many people and crowds who were healed by Jesus. At first, Jesus trained His disciples how to heal, and then He sent them out to do it. In Matthew 10:1 we read of one such example, "And when He had called His twelve disciples to Him, He gave them power over unclean spirits, to cast them out, and to heal all kinds of sickness and all kinds of disease." The question then arises, if Jesus made the way for our healing, why do so many Christians suffer illness, sickness and disease?

Figure 9: Why am I sick?

Starting at the bottom layer in Figure 8, we see that most sicknesses and diseases are rooted in unbelief and a lack of faith. When unbelief and a lack of faith are present, they lead to disobedience to God. God created us to have a relationship with Him. When we choose not to believe, trust or obey Him, it angers Him and it results in curses coming upon us, as we can see in Numbers 14:11-12, "Then the LORD said to Moses: "How long will these people reject Me? And how long will they not believe Me, with all the signs which I have performed among them? I will strike them with the pestilence and disinherit them..." This scripture makes it clear that once rejection takes

136

place that we will suffer consequences such as sickness and poverty.

We have been created with an area inside ourselves where God is supposed to reside. When we accept God and are filled with the Holy Spirit, this area is occupied by the rightful Owner and we know fulfillment. If we do not believe God or we become disobedient toward God, there is a break in the relationship for which we have been created. Unbelief pushes God off the throne in your heart and demonic spirits enter in and compete for the throne. Demons of fear, anxiety and stress also enter in. Our spirit realizes the growing separation between our Father and us, and also recognizes the danger of the darkness we are moving into. The door for foul spirits is then opened in our lives. Unbelief, fear, anxiety and stress are the most common spirits in the causes of sickness and disease.

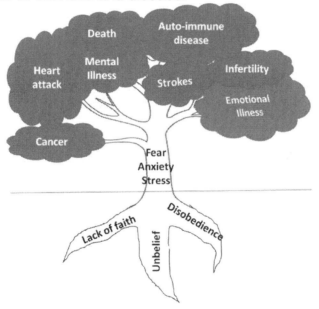

Figure 10: Tree of infirmity

Unbelief is the root of most illnesses. Once unbelief enters it soon opens the door to disobedience and acts of sin. It could probably best be likened to a tree. The roots of the tree would be unbelief, lack of faith and disobedience. The stem of the tree is fear, anxiety and stress and the fruits of the tree are all kinds of sicknesses and diseases. In 1 Thessalonians 4:3-8 it shows the importance of cleaning yourself up spiritually and walking on a path of holiness, "For this is the will of God, your sanctification: ... that each of you should know how to possess his own vessel in sanctification and honor...For God did not call us to uncleanness, but in holiness. Therefore he who rejects this (Own interpretation – deliverance and walking a path of holiness) does not reject man, but God, who has also given us His Holy Spirit."

Disobedience to God results in curses on your life and demon infestation. Those who reject and break covenant with God, do not fall under His protection. They opened the doors to satanic attack and God will step back and allow illness, suffering and poverty to afflict them, in the hope that they will turn back to Him. Unfortunately, these people can also become spiritually blind and deaf. Such people can be lured into a life filled with all kinds of perversity, which could result in infirmities and ultimately physical death.

Bloodline sins also play a role in illness. In Deuteronomy 5:9 God states, "...you shall not bow down to them nor serve them. For I, the LORD your God, am a jealous God, visiting the iniquity of the fathers upon the children to the third and fourth generations of those who hate Me," This scripture shows us clearly that the unrepented sins of our ancestors influence our lives today. This also confirms that you might not have been the one to commit a particular sin, yet because a door was opened to demon infestation when the sin was committed, the demon has the right to infest up to four generations following the person who originally committed the sin. One of the jobs of a demon is to rob you – they love to cause all kinds of illness and pestilence in pursuit of this task.

Directions: Read through each of these statements and rate yourself answering "True" or "False".

Why am I sick?		
	T	F
1	I believe in Jesus		
2	I have full faith that Jesus is going to heal me		
3	I love the Lord with all my heart, all my mind and strength		
4	I have been obedient to God's commandments		
5	I have a personal relationship with the Lord		
6	I hear God's voice		
7	The Bible is true		
8	I do not sin		
9	I have repented for my ancestors' sins		
10	I regularly repented of all my sins		
11	I have used communion in an worthy manner		
12	I have forgiven all who has sinned against me		

Figure 11: Why am I sick?

Here is what your answers reveal about you:

- If your answers were "True" to all the statements:

  Your sickness could possibly be to the glory of God. In John 11:4 we see that Lazarus' sickness was to the glory of God, "When Jesus heard that, He said, "This sickness is not unto death, but for the glory of God, that the Son of God may be glorified through it."" Another example of blindness that was for the glory of God can be seen in John 9:2-3, "And His disciples asked Him, saying, "Rabbi, who sinned, this man or his parents, that he was born blind?" Jesus answered, "Neither this man nor his parents sinned, but that the works of God should be revealed in him.""

- If your answer was "False" to:

Statement 1: I believe in Jesus: You do not believe in Jesus. If you want to be healed by Jesus why not invite Him to reveal Himself to you. The easiest way for you to enjoy an experience and perhaps even receive your healing would be to attend a healing service or find someone who will pray with you for salvation and healing.

Statement 2: I have faith that Jesus will heal me: You need to increase your faith level. Faith is of the utmost importance where healing is concerned. Jesus was moved into healing people when He saw a display of faith. An example of this can be seen in Matthew 9:22, ""But Jesus turned around, and when He saw her He said, "Be of good cheer, daughter; your faith has made you well." And the woman was made well from that hour."

If you need to increase your faith you need to hear the Word of God. Romans 10:17 says, "So then faith comes by hearing, and hearing by the word of God." You build faith by hearing the Word of God, therefore, read your Bible out loud to yourself. Read it daily; remember that this is food to your spiritual man and that your spiritual man needs to eat as regularly as your physical man.

I would also suggest watching shows or meetings where God's supernatural power is manifest. For example, you can try going to Sid Roth's website and watch a couple of his "It's Supernatural" TV shows. This will build hope and faith in you and this pleases God, who is a rewarder of those who diligently seek Him.

Statements 3 or 5: I love the Lord with all my heart, all my mind and strength & I have a personal relationship with the Lord: Your relationship with God has been attacked and you have been robbed by Satan. God has a much deeper and meaningful relationship in mind for you but it is dependent on the choices you make. If you are longing for a deeper and more intimate relationship with God, make the choice to lay down those things which you are putting above Him. These idols

140

might even seem very admirable to you, such as your job, family or function in the church, but their place on your list of priorities should always be after your relationship with God. If you study the Bible, you will notice that God often chastened those He loved with the very idols they worshipped. God never changes. Let's say that you value and spend more time and emotion on your family life than on God. You can expect that your family life will be the very place where God will bring the chastisement. You might find that your work circumstances change to such a degree that you have to travel for work and you are unable to spend the time you would like with your family. God may be using this to help you reorganize your priorities, with Him at the top of the list.

I would like to challenge you to honestly look at the priorities in your heart. Is God first? If not, what have you placed above God? List these things and repent before God for idolatry in your heart. Use our book called "Who are You" to identify those demons which have caused you to fall into idolatry and cast them out according to the steps in the section entitled "The road to Victory". Set God first in your life and you will surely experience a deeper and more meaningful relationship with Him. You will also open the gates for Him to be able to pour out His blessing on your life in the measure He desires.

Statement 4: I have been obedient to God's commandments: The first covenant that God made with man was based on obedience to God's laws and statutes. When people were disobedient to the laws they had to be punished and sin offerings had to be made on their behalf. Jesus came to make a new covenant with us based on love and mercy. It is possible for man to be obedient under this new covenant because the mercy of the Lord covers our sins when we ask for forgiveness.

Forgiveness is a key to receive deliverance and healing. You have to repent and ask forgiveness for all your sins,

141

as well as the sins of your ancestors. You also need to forgive everybody who has sinned against you, from your heart. If you are not able to do this, God cannot forgive you and your healing will not manifest. This becomes clear when you study the Lord's Prayer. To live with unforgiveness in your heart, clearly shows that you still stand in judgment of someone. Now, the Bible says that judgment belongs to Jesus Christ. Jesus is the only man who has not sinned and has earned the right to judge. We have all sinned and have no right to judge one another! To continue with an inability to forgive, in itself, is hypocrisy. By holding someone's weakness against them, you are highlighting your own! What is worse still is that the inability to forgive allows Satan and his demons the right to attack your body with illness. We have, through experience, discovered that the inability to forgive and harboring bitterness, is closely associated to the occurrence of cancer. It is for this reason why we won't minister deliverance to someone who is not willing to forgive.

Statement 6: I hear God's voice: If you cannot hear God's voice, you are not in the relationship God created you to be in with Him. God created us to have a love relationship where we walk and talk constantly. If you do not have this, it means that there is separation and distance between you and God. Separation between you and God leads to fear, anxiety and stress, which in turn leads to sickness.

In order to have a personal relationship with someone you need to have a regular and intimate flow of communication between you. You need to see and hear from this person daily and it needs to be a two way flow of communication. Does your communion with God meet this criteria? Or do you find your prayers hitting the roof and returning to you without accomplishing anything?

Communion with God is imperative to having an intimate relationship with Him. Christian Leadership University has an excellent course that teaches you how to hear God's voice. The course content has been written by Mark Virkler, who trains people to hear God's voice. I highly recommend this course as it helped me and it will help you to walk in intimacy with God. His website is www.cluonline.com.

Statement 7: The Bible is true: In Luke 16:17 Jesus confirms the validity of the law, "And it is easier for heaven and earth to pass away than for one tittle of the law to fail." In Jesus' time the law was the Bible and He confirmed that God was in control of what was in the law to the point of the tiniest mark. This is how I know God – He is involved in the smallest detail. He knows the number of hairs on your head – something you don't even know about yourself. Do you really think that God, who created and maintains everything, would be unable to maintain His written Word to us?

The Bible is the truth, and if you choose to disregard certain parts of it, or add your own interpretation to it, you will be afflicted by the plagues mentioned in the Bible and also lose your salvation. Revelations 22:18-20 gives a clear idea of what happens if you add or take away from the Bible, "For I testify to everyone who hears the words of the prophecy of this book: If anyone adds to these things, God will add to him the plagues that are written in this book; and if anyone takes away from the words of the book of this prophecy, God shall take away his part from the Book of Life, from the holy city, and from the things which are written in this book. He who testifies to these things says, "Surely I am coming quickly." Amen. Even so, come, Lord Jesus!" This scripture makes it clear that you will be afflicted by the plagues mentioned in the Bible if you should add your own interpretation or take away parts of it. If you are truly seeking healing, carefully examine your perception of the Bible. Could this be one of the reasons why you are sick?

Revelation of the Bible and a full understanding of the Scriptures can only be received if you are filled with the Holy Spirit. Let's not rely on our own understanding or our own interpretations, because this has already caused a lot of damage in the churches. We serve the same God; we read the same Bible; we are going to be the same bride to Christ, yet we all follow our own man-made rules and regulations. These rules and regulations are from the pit of hell and they bring division into the body of Christ. They focus man's eyes on earthly matters instead of on God and the work He has commissioned us to do. Allow the Bible to be what you meditate on day and night. It is God's Word and it pleases God when we meditate on His Word. The year 2011 is the Year of Unity, and it is time that those who believe that the Bible is the inerrant Word of God, stand in unity.

If you have erred by adding or taking away from the Bible to suit your own beliefs, way of life, or to be accepted into certain societies or circles, repent and ask God's forgiveness. Ask the Lord to remove the plagues from you, through the price paid by Jesus on the cross.

Statement 8, 9, and 10: I do not sin; I have repented for my ancestors' sins; I always repent of my sins. 1 John 1:8 says, "If we say that we have no sin, we deceive ourselves, and the truth is not in us." We all sin and it leads to open doors for demons to afflict us with sickness and poverty. Ask the Holy Spirit to reveal the unrepented sins of your ancestors to you. Repent of these sins on their behalf and ask the Lord to forgive them and lift any curses off you and your children, which have come upon you as a result of their sins.

Statement 11: I always use communion in a worthy manner. If you have not confessed your sins or have failed to forgive others their sins before taking communion, you have received a curse from God over your health. 1 Corinthians 11:27-30 shows that taking communion in an unworthy manner will cause sickness and leads to death, "Therefore whoever eats this bread or drinks this cup of the Lord in an unworthy manner will be guilty of the body and blood of the Lord. But let a man examine himself, and so let him eat of the bread and drink of the cup. For he who eats and drinks in an unworthy manner eats and drinks judgment to himself, not discerning the Lord's body. For this reason many are weak and sick among you, and many sleep."

It is important to confess this sin before the Lord and purpose in your heart not to do it again. Ask the Lord to forgive you and lift every curse of sickness that He has brought over you.

Statement 12: I have forgiven all who have sinned against me. We are also expected to forgive others. Matthew 6:12 says, "And forgive us our debts, as we forgive our debtors." According to this short piece of scripture, we are required to forgive others and we will be forgiven in the same measure that we offer forgiveness. Someone seeking healing must be willing to forgive anyone who sinned against them or hurt them in any way.

A spirit of blame and unforgiveness can stand between you and your healing. It is crucial to forgive others so that you may be forgiven for the sins you have committed. Matthew 6:14-15 says, "For if you forgive men their trespasses, your heavenly Father will also forgive you. But if you do not forgive men their trespasses, neither will your Father forgive your trespasses." We will not attempt to cast demons out of someone who does not forgive and speak it out.

Many people find it difficult to forgive others. They are so caught up in the pain of their memories and often the unfairness of what happened to them, that they fail to see the damage that the unforgiveness causes them. Unforgiveness stems from hardness of heart and leads to bitterness, revenge, hatred and even murder. On the other hand, the person who harbors the unforgiveness is poisoned from the inside. Unforgiveness opens the door to a horde of demons and a lot of them will cause sickness, plagues and poverty to abound in your life.

If you have harbored unforgiveness you have to realize that judgment belongs to God. While you are unable to forgive somebody for what they have done to you, you are standing in judgment, and God will stand back. Forgive this person for the sake of your own wellbeing. Allow God to be the judge in the situation and turn the person over to God to deal with – not with a heart filled with hatred and revenge, but with the knowledge that you are also a sinner and that all of us are very grateful that God shows us mercy and allows us to turn from sin to His goodness.

The statements in the last questionnaire and subsequent discussions would have identified reasons for why your healing has not yet manifested. In summary some of the reasons could be:

- You do not believe in Jesus Christ
- You, or those who are praying for you, lack faith in Jesus that He can heal you
- You, or your ancestors, have unrepented sins that needs to be dealt with
- You have allowed separation between you and God and demons have taken up the place inside of you which is reserved for God
- You have sinned and curses of God have been unleashed upon you
- You have partaken of communion without being in right standing with God and brought curses of God upon yourself
- You have added or taken away from the Bible which has brought curses of God upon you

- You have not kept God's commandments or statutes and have brought curses of God upon yourself, as well as opened the door for demons to infest you
- You have failed to forgive others which results in your sins not being forgiven

If any of these reasons are applicable to you, they must first be dealt with in order for your healing to manifest.

Let us spend some time and examine Jesus in action when He healed others. Examining Biblical examples provides us with guidelines on how to successfully heal others.

Jesus heals the man with the withered hand

Matthew 12:10-15 says, "And behold, there was a man who had a withered hand. And they asked Him, saying, "Is it lawful to heal on the Sabbath?"--that they might accuse Him. Then He said to them, "What man is there among you who has one sheep, and if it falls into a pit on the Sabbath, will not lay hold of it and lift it out? Of how much more value then is a man than a sheep? Therefore it is lawful to do good on the Sabbath." Then He said to the man, "Stretch out your hand." And he stretched it out, and it was restored as whole as the other. Then the Pharisees went out and plotted against Him, how they might destroy Him. But when Jesus knew it, He withdrew from there. And great multitudes followed Him, and He healed them all."

What can we learn from this example?
- The Pharisees tried to use their own interpretation of the laws to show that Jesus broke the law of God. If they were able to accuse Him successfully, they would be able to judge Him and prove that His claims to be God are false
- You can expect that those with the spirit of religion will persecute you when you heal people through the Spirit of God, just like the Pharisees tried to destroy Jesus

147

- Jesus was not afraid to expose the false accusations and beliefs of the church leadership of His time. We should follow His example – men are not infallible

- Jesus was not afraid to heal even though the church leadership tried to find a reason to accuse Him. Jesus chose to be obedient to God and to do the work that God sent Him to accomplish. We should do the same despite resistance from others

- The Pharisees confronted Jesus openly but they also plotted against Him behind His back. We can expect the same; there will be times that you will be directly confronted but most of the time the attack will be underhanded. Stay vigilant and pray for God's protection day and night

- Please note that Jesus knew what was happening and withdrew from there. God will not force Himself on others, especially not those who resist Him – He will withdraw. We should do the same. If church leaders choose to resist the Lord, withdraw from them and those who choose to follow them. God will never force Himself on anybody and neither should we force God on anyone

- Even though Jesus chose to withdraw from the presence of the church leadership, great multitudes still followed Him. This is a very encouraging scripture for leaders who serve under ungodly church leadership. Withdraw from those who resist God and God will add to your ministry those who seek Him in truth and Spirit

- Note that Jesus healed all who followed Him. Let us minister to all those who are choosing to seek healing and deliverance from Jesus. Jesus says that we will be recognized by these signs as His followers

Jesus gives instructions for the sick

James 5:14-16 says, "Is anyone among you sick? Let him call for the elders of the church, and let them pray over him, anointing him with oil in the name of the Lord. And the prayer of faith will save the sick,

148

and the Lord will raise him up. And if he has committed sins, he will be forgiven. Confess your trespasses to one another, and pray for one another, that you may be healed. The effective, fervent prayer of a righteous man avails much."

What can we learn from this example?

- Healing should be a normal part of church life. Jesus told the people to call for the elders of the church to anoint them for healing. It is surprising how many people go to strangers they don't know at all when they are desperate for healing. This is very dangerous because Satan is also into the healing business – he imitates everything God does. The only difference is that people who pray for healing through any other means but the Holy Spirit, do so with the assistance of demonic spirits. These spirits will oust spirits of illness but replace them with other, stronger spirits, which will claim the person's life and soul. Such a person will seem healed but could soon afterward die of another unrelated illness or tragedy. We have to test the spirit before we allow anybody to pray for us. The Bible warns us not to allow anyone to lay hands on you hastily. It is dangerous, because a transfer of demonic spirits will take place

- It is the responsibility of the elders to understand how to pray for healing and to flow in God's anointing to manifest the healing. It is not the sole responsibility of the pastor to pray for healing. Pastors should equip the members of their congregations to do the work. It is a sure sign of insecurity and disobedience to God if a pastor is the only person praying for healing and deliverance

- We are told to pray for healing and to anoint them with oil in the name of the Lord. Our request for healing is made to the One who paid the price for it – Jesus. We pray for healing under the anointing of the Holy Spirit and the anointing oil is a symbol of the work of the Holy Spirit. We pray in the name of the Lord Jesus Christ because He has already overcome the enemy and has given us the right and authority to do so in His name

Paul teaches that sin causes sickness

Romans 6:19 says, "I speak in human terms because of the weakness (Illness, disease, infirmity or sickness) of your flesh. For just as you presented your members as slaves of uncleanness, and of lawlessness leading to more lawlessness, so now present your members as slaves of righteousness for holiness."

What can we learn from this example?

- The word "weakness" in this scripture could also be translated as illness, disease, infirmity or sickness. Here Paul says that we are slaves to sin and that is why we are sick. He encourages us to walk a path of holiness by living righteous lives

- Paul encourages us to live holy. In order to do so, all the unclean spirits who have occupied us while we lived a sinful life, must be cast out. Going through deliverance is a jumpstart on the path of holiness. Being washed by the Word (have the Bible read aloud in your presence) will also cleanse you over time

Paul boasted in his sickness

1 Corinthians 2:3-5 says, "I was with you in weakness, in fear, and in much trembling. And my speech and my preaching were not with persuasive words of human wisdom, but in demonstration of the Spirit and of power, that your faith should not be in the wisdom of men but in the power of God."

What can we learn from this example?

- Paul admitted his personal sickness and weakness to those he ministered to. He encouraged them to focus their eyes on the Lord as the perfect example, and not on man, who is still walking a path of holiness

- Our faith should never be in men but in God – it is God who does the healing, we are merely obedient to pray

- I've never seen a person be convinced of the truth of the Bible through the wisdom displayed by man. It is good to have wisdom and we have to grow in knowledge, but that is not going to save souls or heal people. Only God can do that through the working of His Holy Spirit within us. We believe with our hearts – not with our minds! Allow the Holy Spirit to minister through you; it is the only effective way to save souls

- Paul was probably one of the greatest Evangelists who have ever existed, yet he boasted in his infirmities. 2 Corinthians 12:9 says, "And He said to me, "My grace is sufficient for you, for My strength is made perfect in weakness." Therefore most gladly I will rather boast in my infirmities, that the power of Christ may rest upon me."

- If you wish to minister Gods healing to people successfully, please remember to clearly mention that you have no power to heal but that God has this power. It's important that those who come to you for healing don't place their faith or hope on you. This is a trap of Satan to bring you to a fall and to bring disgrace to God's work. Let us walk in humbleness, always keeping our own weaknesses in mind

Paul heals the lame

Acts 3:6-7 says, "Then Peter said, "Silver and gold I do not have, but what I do have I give you: In the name of Jesus Christ of Nazareth, rise up and walk." And he took him by the right hand and lifted him up, and immediately his feet and ankle bones received strength."

What can we learn from this example?
- We will be asked for material goods but we may give those people something that has even more value

- Jesus, nor His disciples, ever gave money to those following them or seeking ministry. They gave them something more valuable – something that cannot be bought. They gave them deliverance and healing, both physical and spiritual

- Peter prayed in the name of Jesus Christ, leaving us with the correct example of how to pray and receive healing – through Jesus Christ

- Peter took the lame man by his right hand and lifted him. This shows that the healing did not manifest yet because the man would have gotten up by himself. It took an act of faith on Peters' part to allow the healing to manifest. It says that as soon as Peter lifted the man up that his bones and feet were strengthened. We must keep our eyes on the Lord and His abilities and not on the physical around us. If the Lord showed you that the healing would manifest, He is not a liar. His word will go forth and accomplish what it has set out to do – this is a matter of faith. You have to have the guts to believe God!

- The Scriptures also say that our faith is displayed by our works. The healing was spoken out by Peter (he spoke out what he believed was God's intention) and then he had to perform an action. In our day we could look for operations or physical therapy for someone who is lame, but it took something from Peter to do what he did – something that did not involve the human mind. Peter had to listen to what God was saying to him concerning His will for this man, and then Peter had to build up the courage to do what God told or showed him to do. Peter then had to take an action in public that others would probably call crazy – to lift a lame man to his feet. To pray for someone's healing takes faith and guts. Don't give up! The disciples walked with Jesus for years before they had what it took

Casting out demons results in healing

Acts 8:7 says, "For unclean spirits, crying with a loud voice, came out of many who were possessed; and many who were paralyzed and lame were healed."

What can we learn from this example?

- Healing and deliverance go hand in hand. When deliverance takes place, healing usually follows. If God shows you that you are dealing with an illness caused by a demonic entity, you also need to commune with God to find out if it is His will and timing for the person's healing to manifest. Once God gives you the go-ahead, you should already be rejoicing, because the word of victory has already gone forth from God's throne, and the Bible states that God's Word will always accomplish that which it sets out to do

- Demons often manifest when they are cast out. Demons may plead, curse or cry out when you chase them out. They may refuse to leave, yet with persistent use of the name and authority of Jesus, they have to submit and leave

- All the signs that Jesus mentioned in Mark 16:17 were visible in His disciples. They cast out demons, they spoke in new tongues, they prayed for the sick and they were healed, they took up serpents, and they drank cups of poison and were not harmed by it

Ananias prays for Saul's healing

Acts 9:17-18 says, "And Ananias went his way and entered the house; and laying his hands on him he said, "Brother Saul, the Lord Jesus, who appeared to you on the road as you came, has sent me that you may receive your sight and be filled with the Holy Spirit." Immediately there fell from his eyes something like scales, and he received his sight at once; and he arose and was baptized."

153

What can we learn from this example?

- The laying on of hands is scriptural

- Healing is guaranteed when you've been commissioned by the Lord to do so. It's important to pray and possibly fast prior to praying for healing. This ensures that you press into the presence of the Lord and know His heart concerning the healing. It's often during this time that God will give you revelation of what you are dealing with, and what He would like you to do during the session

- The Lord gave Ananias a word of knowledge to share with Saul. Ananias shared it with Saul and this gave Saul assurance that Ananias was sent to him by the Lord. The word also built Saul's faith for the healing that had to take place

- Physical manifestation of the healing took place – scales fell from his eyes

- He received immediate healing

- He immediately took a step of obedience – to be baptized

- There is usually a parallel relationship between the spiritual and physical. Saul's spiritual eyes were also opened at the same time. For the first time, he saw the importance of baptism and took this step of obedience. Healing is not just something that stands alone. It is an act of love and mercy by God that deserves a deeper level of commitment from the recipient to a relationship with Him. This truth should be a burning desire within those who have experienced a healing by God. As a minister of God this heart's attitude should not be exploited. Be extremely careful that this experience does not end up being a test to you and that you be found weak in areas before God. The glory of what took place belongs to God; do not wallow in it, as if you have affected the healing. Furthermore, be careful about accepting payment from the person who was healed, if offered. Make sure that you obtain God's approval before excepting anything

Paul laid hands on Publius' father and healed him

Acts 28:8-9 says, "And it happened that the father of Publius lay sick of a fever and dysentery. Paul went in to him and prayed, and he laid his hands on him and healed him. So when this was done, the rest of those on the island who had diseases also came and were healed."

What can we learn from this example?

- All kinds of illness are healed through the laying on of hands

- Once a healing has taken place, the word will spread and faith will be stirred up in many other ill people who will come for prayer. This is a good time to remember that you are only a vessel through whom God works and that you are not the one who is effecting the healing. Remember your dependence on God and constantly seek His counsel. Remain humble and enjoy the privilege of being in God's presence and seeing Him at work!

Jesus heals various diseases

Luke 4:38-42 says, "Now He arose from the synagogue and entered Simon's house. But Simon's wife's mother was sick with a high fever, and they made request of Him concerning her. So He stood over her and rebuked the fever, and it left her. And immediately she arose and served them. When the sun was setting, all those who had any that were sick with various diseases brought them to Him; and He laid His hands on every one of them and healed them. And demons also came out of many, crying out and saying, "You are the Christ, the Son of God!" And He, rebuking them, did not allow them to speak, for they knew that He was the Christ.

Now when it was day, He departed and went into a deserted place. And the crowd sought Him and came to Him, and tried to keep Him from leaving them".

What can we learn from this example?

- Jesus rebuked the fever and she was healed. Once again, deliverance and healing go hand in hand. Demons often cause illness and once they are cast out the afflicted are healed

- When a healing takes place the word will spread and many others will come to be healed as well

- There is a great variety of diseases that can be healed through prayer

- Demons often manifest when cast out during prayers for healing. Do not attempt to enter into conversations with the demons unnecessarily, they are by nature liars and deceivers and will try their best to retain their ground in the afflicted person

- Once the Lord uses you in healing His children, the demand of the crowds on you can become overwhelming. It is important to have a balance – you still need to maintain Godly priorities in your life. God first, your spouse second, your family third and your work (even if it is God's work) fourth. You must regularly separate yourself unto God and fill up in His presence. God will never expect you to work yourself to a standstill – that is the work of Satan and also amount to striving. Even Jesus took some time out to fill up with His Father. God was in charge before you were born and His work will continue when you are gone

Jesus heals a leper

Luke 5:12-14 says, "And it happened when He was in a certain city, that behold, a man who was full of leprosy saw Jesus; and he fell on his face and implored Him, saying, "Lord, if You are willing, You can make me clean." Then He put out His hand and touched him, saying, "I am willing; be cleansed." Immediately the leprosy left him. And He charged him to tell no one, "But go and show yourself to the priest, and make an offering for your cleansing, as a testimony to them, just as Moses commanded.""

What can we learn from this example?

- This man was an outcast of society yet even the outcasts hope in and have faith for their healing through Jesus. No sin or illness can be so bad or big that Jesus will turn you away

- This man fell on his face and implored Jesus. I would say that he was calling out to Jesus for His healing from his heart. What is the motivation and attitude of those whom you want to pray for? Jesus responded to this man who knew that without Gods' intervention, he would be doomed for the rest of his existence

- This man stated his faith in Jesus by saying that if Jesus was willing, that He could heal him. He recognized that Jesus had the power to heal, but he also knew to approach the Lord with humility

- Jesus told him not to tell anyone, except that he should comply with the laws in order for him to be declared clean and to be able to enter society again. Why do you think Jesus told him not to tell anyone? Could it be that Jesus was tired? The verses that follow tell us a different story. Luke 5:15-16 says, "...the report went around concerning Him all the more; and great multitudes came together to hear, and to be healed by Him of their infirmities. So He, Himself often withdrew into the wilderness and prayed."

- One of the reasons Jesus kept asking those who were healed not to say anything was because the crowds were flocking to Jesus, not because of who He was, but because of what He could do for them. We still tend to do this with God today; instead of entering into a love relationship with Him, we try to use Him for our own benefit. God's heart towards us is filled with love and compassion and when we ask Him for healing He often complies despite our heart's intentions. Remember to share God's motivation for healing with those you minister to. Encourage them to enter into a deeper love relationship with the Lord. Let us not tire the Lord, but let us add to His joy by ensuring that those we minister to, enter into a deeper love relationship with Him.

Jesus heals the lame

Luke 5:17-21 says, "Now it happened on a certain day, as He was teaching, that there were Pharisees and teachers of the law sitting by, who had come out of every town of Galilee, Judea, and Jerusalem. And the power of the Lord was present to heal them. Then behold, men brought on a bed a man who was paralyzed, whom they sought to bring in and lay before Him. And when they could not find how they might bring him in, because of the crowd, they went up on the housetop and let him down with his bed through the tiling into the midst before Jesus. When He saw their faith, He said to him, "Man, your sins are forgiven you." And the scribes and the Pharisees began to reason, saying, "Who is this who speaks blasphemies? Who can forgive sins but God alone?"".

What can we learn from this example?

- In this scripture Jesus was teaching others, including the Pharisees. The anointing to heal is often present when you train others. Training is not just the conveyance of information but the opportunity for practical application of what is being taught

- Faith pleases God and where faith is present, healing often breaks through

- Jesus has the authority to forgive sin. This fact happened to be a stumbling block for the church leaders. Some churches these days believe that you have to pay money or do good deeds in order for your sins to be forgiven. This is not what Jesus taught. Jesus said that we have to forgive others and ask for forgiveness of our own sins, in order to be forgiven. As soon as Jesus forgave this man his sins, he was healed.

So how do we apply this when we pray for healing? We need to help the people identify their sins and the unrepented sins of their ancestors; lead them in prayers of repentance and lead them in prayers of forgiveness toward all who sinned against them. This takes away the rights of the demons who have afflicted them and caused the illness within. It becomes much easier to cast these demons out once they have lost their rights to inhabit a person

Jesus calls the sinners to repentance

Luke 5:31-32 says, "Jesus answered and said to them, "Those who are well have no need of a physician, but those who are sick. I have not come to call the righteous, but sinners, to repentance.""

What can we learn from this example?

- Jesus said that He did not come for the healing of those who think that they are well. If you think that you have no sin but you are suffering illness, chances are good that you will not receive healing from God. There are a couple of things that cause illness of which sin is the main reason. Sin of your ancestors and your own sin are the most likely causes for your illness. There are exceptional cases where an illness is to the glory of God

- What is the attitude of the person you want to pray for? Are they totally willing to confess sins or are they maintaining their own righteousness? If you pray for a person who claims to be righteous and is not willing to confess their sins, no healing will break through. Jesus, Himself, said that He did not come to call the righteous to repentance. Without repentance there will be no healing!

Jesus heals a multitude of people

Luke 6:17-19 says, "And He came down with them and stood on a level place with a crowd of His disciples and a great multitude of people from all Judea and Jerusalem, and from the seacoast of Tyre and Sidon, who came to hear Him and be healed of their diseases, as well as those who were tormented with unclean spirits. And they were healed. And the whole multitude sought to touch Him, for power went out from Him and healed them all."

What can we learn from this example?

- Healing is a display of power by God. People can feel this power. The people tried to touch Him because they felt the power of God which manifested healing. When you minister healing you will feel the power of God flow through you; you will know when it is present to heal. Minister and teach the afflicted until you feel God's power, or as we also call it, the anointing of the Holy Spirit, upon you before you pray for healing

Jesus heals a woman with flow of blood

Mark 5:24-34 says, "So Jesus went with him, and a great multitude followed Him and thronged Him. Now a certain woman had a flow of blood for twelve years, and had suffered many things from many physicians. She had spent all that she had and was no better, but rather grew worse.

When she heard about Jesus, she came behind Him in the crowd and touched His garment. For she said, "If only I may touch His clothes, I shall be made well." Immediately the fountain of her blood was dried up, and she felt in her body that she was healed of the affliction. And Jesus, immediately knowing in Himself that power had gone out of Him, turned around in the crowd and said, "Who touched My clothes?" But His disciples said to Him, "You see the multitude thronging You, and You say, 'Who touched Me?' " And He looked around to see her who had done this thing. But the woman, fearing and trembling, knowing what had happened to her, came and fell down before Him and told Him the whole truth. And He said to her, "Daughter, your faith has made you well. Go in peace, and be healed of your affliction."

What can we learn from this example?

- An illness that cannot be healed by doctors can be healed by the Lord. This woman had been sick for 12 years and had lost most of what she had in an effort to obtain her health from doctors. We have found that nothing is too difficult for the Lord to heal. It is at the point where doctors give up that the Lord likes to perform miracles

- A high level of faith in Jesus can manifest your healing. Jesus did not pray for this woman but she believed that if she could merely touch His cloak, she would be healed. This is in line with Matthew 9:29 where Jesus said, "According to your faith let it be to you"

- Healing manifests through power. Jesus perceived power going out from Him. This is a wonderful example of a deliverance which takes place because of the strong faith of a woman in the healing ability of Jesus. The woman was immediately healed from her affliction

Jesus gives His disciples power to cure diseases

Luke 9:1-6 says, "Then He called His twelve disciples together and gave them power and authority over all demons, and to cure diseases. He sent them to preach the kingdom of God and to heal the sick. And He said to them, "Take nothing for the journey, neither staffs nor bag nor bread nor money; and do not have two tunics apiece. Whatever house you enter, stay there, and from there depart. And whoever will not receive you, when you go out of that city, shake off the very dust from your feet as a testimony against them." So they departed and went through the towns, preaching the gospel and healing everywhere."

161

What can we learn from this example?

- This scripture clearly states that we have the power and the authority to cure diseases

- Jesus gave his disciples the commission to heal the sick and so do all those who follow Jesus

- Jesus gave His disciples command not to make any provision for their trip. It is important for us to hear God's voice even concerning our everyday needs, such as food and clothes. When you work for someone you receive your reward for the work you do. When you work for God, He will provide all your needs. You have to make sure that when you go out to do God's work, that you've communed with the "Boss" and that you are in line with what He wants to do. Even in secular work, payment is not made for work done outside of the scope

- Jesus also gave the following practical commands:

  - Speak peace over a house you enter. Luke 10:5-6 says, "But whatever house you enter, first say, 'Peace to this house.' And if a son of peace is there, your peace will rest on it; if not, it will return to you."

  - Remain in the same house. Luke 10:7 says, "And remain in the same house, eating and drinking such things as they give, for the laborer is worthy of his wages. Do not go from house to house."

  - Eat what is set before you. Luke 10:8 says, "Whatever city you enter, and they receive you, eat such things as are set before you."

- Jesus commanded the disciples to shake the dust from their feet as a testimony against those who would not receive them. What an awesome scripture – dust will testify against those who do not receive God! This scripture tells us that we are not to remain in a place where the people are resisting God. Instead we are to leave and then perform a prophetic action that will serve as a testimony against them. In the Day of Judgment, this dust will testify against these people that they did not

162

accept the message brought by those who share the Gospel. These people will stand guilty before God and will receive their judgment

Jesus heals an epileptic boy

Luke 9:38-42 says, "Suddenly a man from the multitude cried out, saying, "Teacher, I implore You, look on my son, for he is my only child. And behold, a spirit seizes him, and he suddenly cries out; it convulses him so that he foams at the mouth; and it departs from him with great difficulty, bruising him. So I implored Your disciples to cast it out, but they could not." Then Jesus answered and said, "O faithless and perverse generation, how long shall I be with you and bear with you? Bring your son here." And as he was still coming, the demon threw him down and convulsed him. Then Jesus rebuked the unclean spirit, healed the child, and gave him back to his father."

What can we learn from this example?

- Convulsions, seizures and epilepsy are often caused by demons. This is good news because it means that deliverance will bring healing

- Where there is a lack of faith or faithlessness, no healing will take place

- Where there is perversity, no healing will take place. The root word for perverse is to "turn away". This implies that the disciples were taught how to cast out demons and to heal but they turned away from what they were taught. Perverse also means "corrupt" which indicates that the disciples were not pure but still had sins that they were dealing with. In this example, being faithless meant that the disciples did not trust or believe that God had the power or ability to deliver and heal this boy. Once again the principle in Matthew 9:29 applies, which says, "Then He touched their eyes, saying, "According to your faith let it be to you."" Our faith in God when we pray for healing must be strong, otherwise healing will not take place

163

- Jesus first cast out the demon before He healed him. When we minister to people we also first cast the demons out, rob them of the territory they occupied within the person, and then we pray for healing

Jesus heals a mute

Luke 11:14 says, "And He was casting out a demon, and it was mute. So it was, when the demon had gone out, that the mute spoke; and the multitudes marveled."

What can we learn from this example?
- Jesus cast the mute demon out and when the demon left, the healing manifested. Healing often takes place as soon as the demon has been cast out

Fear, anxiety and stress accomplished nothing

Luke 12:25-26, 29-31 says, "And which of you by worrying can add one cubit to his stature? If you then are not able to do the least, why are you anxious for the rest?...And do not seek what you should eat or what you should drink, nor have an anxious mind. For all these things the nations of the world seek after, and your Father knows that you need these things. But seek the kingdom of God, and all these things shall be added to you."

What can we learn from this example?
- Fear, anxiety and stress are the root causes of most illnesses. In this scripture Jesus shows us the futility of stress and anxiety – it accomplishes nothing good. If you are disobedient and allow these thoughts to assail your mind and these demons to enter your body, they open the door to hoards of other demons which cause illness and poverty and death

- Jesus tells us not to be anxious concerning our daily needs, such as what we should eat or drink; instead He tells us to seek the kingdom of God and that if we do this, God will take care of our daily needs. We, as God's children, need to learn to take our focus off the physical and put it on the spiritual. We have been created to have a deep, loving relationship with God, and God is spiritual. Do you want your physical needs taken care of? Then seek the kingdom of God and God says that He will take care of our daily needs

- If you are afflicted with illness and you recognize the fruits of fear, anxiety and stress in your life, chances are good that these demons need to be cast out of you. You can start off by asking God forgiveness for harboring fear, anxiety and stress. Further information on how to do deliverance can be found in our book called "Who are You" which is available from Amazon.com, Xulon Press and on order from any bookstore

- In Luke 12:4-5, Jesus had the following to say about fear, "And I say to you, My friends, do not be afraid of those who kill the body, and after that have no more that they can do. But I will show you whom you should fear: Fear Him who, after He has killed, has power to cast into hell; yes, I say to you, fear Him!"

Fear is experienced when your senses send information to your brain, which is interpreted by your brain as a threat. Chemicals are released into your body with messages to your body to fight the danger or flee from it. In other words, if what you see, hear, smell, taste or feel is perceived as dangerous, your body will react on chemicals released from the brain. There is a twofold reaction, a physical one, which is almost automatic, and which helps you to react in times of physical danger; and an emotional one, which has the potential to cause a lot of damage to your body, soul and spirit. The danger with emotional fear is that the actual object of fear need not be present for the release of the "fear" chemicals into the body. This means that a mere thought triggers a harmful chemical release into the body. When this happens frequently it leads to all kinds of serious illness or even death.

Satan's prediction of your future has the potential to cause ungodly fear. If you believe the rumors he brings to your ears, or the circumstances he surrounds you with, or the pictures he paints in your mind, it will become the reality in future. The Bible confirms this in Deuteronomy 28:60, "Moreover He will bring back on you all the diseases of Egypt, of which you were afraid, and they shall cling to you." Fear is the opposite of faith and trust. God calls us to walk in faith and trust in Him. He often encourages us with prophecy or promises so we believe and move forward in that which He has called us to do. If you have a promise or prophecy from God, write it down, meditate on it and stand on it until it comes into fruition. Joshua 1:9 says, "Have I not commanded you? Be strong and of good courage; do not be afraid, nor be dismayed, for the LORD your God is with you wherever you go."

Jesus heals a man's ear

Luke 22:50-51 says, "And one of them struck the servant of the high priest and cut off his right ear. But Jesus answered and said, "Permit even this." And He touched his ear and healed him."

What can we learn from this example?
- Even in physical warfare there is room for God to heal wounds. Who would think that God can also be found on the battlefield? Yet at this moment in time, while they were arresting Him, in the fray of the moment one of them was injured. Jesus healed this man who had come out against Him. Please note that Jesus' betrayers were the church leadership of that time. Let us always keep our eye open for an opportunity that God wants to use to His glory

- Jesus healed this man with a single touch. Jesus had been in deep intercessory prayer for most of the night prior to this healing taking place. If you live in God's presence, this could become a normal part of your day

Paul heals in miraculous ways

Acts 5:15-16 says, "...so that they brought the sick out into the streets and laid them on beds and couches, that at least the shadow of Peter passing by might fall on some of them. Also a multitude gathered from the surrounding cities to Jerusalem, bringing sick people and those who were tormented by unclean spirits, and they were all healed."

What can we learn from this example?
- Paul's healing ministry was exceptional. He walked in the miraculous yet he never claimed to be wise or perfect. He is a great example to all of us who follow Jesus. In Acts 19:11-12 it says, "Now God worked unusual miracles by the hands of Paul, so that even handkerchiefs or aprons were brought from his body to the sick, and the diseases left them and the evil spirits went out of them." We must not place God in a box where healing is concerned. God is creative and loves to do new and wonderful healings

How to pray for healing

Most illnesses are rooted in unbelief, lack of faith in God and disobedience to God's laws and statutes. Once these roots are established in a person's life, it give way to all kinds of active sins. It is this break in the love relationship between man and God, disobedience to God, and sins that cause the curses and illnesses of Egypt (Deuteronomy 28) to afflict a person.

Sins of your ancestors which have not been confessed and repented of, often cause illnesses in later generations. Identifying the root causes of the illnesses, as well as the demons that have entered the person, must take place. This must be followed by prayers of repentance in order for forgiveness to be received and healing to take place.

It is important to seek God's face before praying for healing so that you can find God's will for the person seeking healing. God is the One who does the healing and if healing is not in God's will, your prayers will not be effective. You therefore have to spend time in fasting and prayer to find out what God is busy with in the person's life. Once you have a commission from God to pray for healing, you may go ahead.

Healing and deliverance often go hand in hand. You might have to do deliverance before praying for the healing to manifest. Please refer to Chapter 4 for guidelines on how to cast out a demon.

To pray for healing, the following guidelines can be used:
- Pray and fast beforehand if required to do so by the Holy Spirit
- Invite the Holy Spirit to take charge of the session. Listen to the Holy Spirit throughout the session and do and say only that which He permits you to do
- Create an atmosphere where God is present by worshipping and praising God
- Share testimonies that will increase the level of faith of those present
- You must be experiencing the healing power or anointing of God present
- Be directed by the Holy Spirit and do as He tells you to do
- Lead the person in prayers of repentance and forgiveness
- Ensure that the person has forgiven all who have sinned against them
- Use anointing oil to anoint the person, if directed to do so by the Holy Spirit
- Lay your hands on the person, if directed to do so by the Holy Spirit

- Ask God for healing for the person and pray prayers as led by the Holy Spirit
- Perform any prophetic actions as directed by the Holy Spirit
- Persist in prayer until the healing manifests
- Command the affected body parts to submit to the authority of the Lord and to be healed
- Thank the Lord for the healing
- Caution the person not to fall back into sin but instead to aggressively pursue a deep love relationship with the Lord
- For an intimate relationship to be established and maintained between a person and God, it is imperative that there is two way communication. It is therefore very important to make sure that the person you have ministered to can hear God's voice. I advise those I minister to, to complete the course of "How to hear God's voice" presented by Mark Virkler, available at the following website: www.cluonline.com

Conclusion

Conclusion

Jesus gave us signs by which we will be identified and by which we can identify others as His followers. In order to flow in these signs we need to believe in Jesus and be filled with the Holy Spirit.

To flow in these signs is to step into the realm of the supernatural. It is a path where you follow in the footsteps of Jesus, casting out demons, speaking in heavenly languages, healing the sick, taking up serpents and enjoying God's divine protection. These footsteps of Jesus lead us on paths of victory over sin, sickness and oppression. They lead us out of prison cells on paths of holiness, where we take up the reigns of rulership which our Father has entrusted into our hands. And when the day of reckoning comes, the same footsteps will safely lead us through Heaven's Gates where the Lord will personally welcome us into His arms and His Kingdom.

These signs will lead you into a love relationship with the Lord, one that will not fail you the day you meet Jesus face to face. On that day, you will see His face light up in recognition as He welcomes you home.

Made in the USA
San Bernardino, CA
06 July 2016